LANGTANG, GOSAINKUND & HELAMBU

A TREKKER'S GUIDE

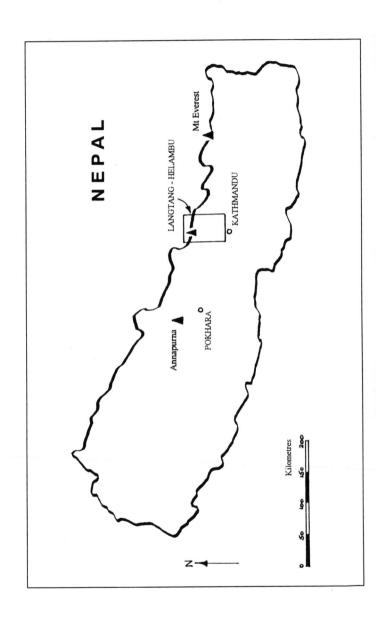

NEPAL

LANGTANG - HELAMBU

Mt Everest

Annapurna

POKHARA

KATHMANDU

N

Kilometres

0   50   100   150   200

LANGTANG, GOSAINKUND & HELAMBU
A TREKKER'S GUIDE

by

Kev Reynolds

CICERONE PRESS
MILNTHORPE, CUMBRIA, UK

This book is for Kirken Sherpa and Uttar Kumar Rai, 'Amit' - with thanks

ACKNOWLEDGEMENTS

The help, advice and encouragement of a number of people made the task of researching and writing this guide an enjoyable and much easier one than might otherwise have been. Others shared trails, tea-houses and lodges along the way, added to my own observations and increased the pleasures of being on trek. To each one I offer my gratitude. They include all at Cicerone Press for their continued support and for yet again providing me with an excuse to spend many weeks wandering in the Himalaya. Alan Payne, long-time climbing and trekking partner, trekked the trails with me and once again proved to be a first-rate companion. Roland Hiss, whose personal experience of Langtang dates back many years, came up with welcome advice at an early stage; while the company and enthusiasm of Ralph Wildgans and Isabelle Löwenthal from Vienna were a real joy for much of the way. A special word of thanks is reserved for 'our man in Kathmandu' - Kirken Sherpa of Mt Kailash Paradise Trekking, whom I first met in the Ötztal Alps of Austria, and who subsequently took care of all pre-trek arrangements, reduced the bureaucratic hassles of Kathmandu, and introduced us to Amit, our porter-guide who did so much to educate us to the real Nepal. Amit, of course, deserves special praise and deep gratitude. Final word of thanks must go to my wife who once again kept the home together while I roamed the trails of Nepal. Her loving support made it possible.

Kev Reynolds

Cicerone Guides by the same author:

Annapurna - a Trekker's Guide	Central Switzerland
Everest - a Trekker's Guide	Alpine Pass Route
Walks & Climbs in the Pyrenees	Chamonix to Zermatt - the Walker's Haute Route
Walks in the Engadine - Switzerland	The Wealdway & The Vanguard Way
The Valais	The South Downs Way & The Downs Link
The Jura (with R.B. Evans)	The Cotswold Way
The Bernese Alps	Walking in Kent Vols I & II
Ticino	

Front Cover: Gangchempo, Tilman's 'Fluted Peak', soars over the valley, as seen here from the Langtang Khola below Kyangjin. (p.95)

CONTENTS

ADVICE TO READERS

Readers are advised that whilst every effort is taken by the author to ensure the accuracy of this guidebook, changes can occur which may affect the contents. It is advisable to check locally on transport, accommodation, shops, etc. but even rights of way can be altered and, more especially overseas, paths can be eradicated by landslip, forest fires or changes of ownership.

The publishers would welcome notes of any such changes.

PREFACE

Unbelievably high, and with a beauty that defies description, mountains of the Himalaya dominate northern Nepal. Seen from the air they hang confused among the clouds. Glimpsed from the Kathmandu Valley they form a remote horizon. From the foothills they tease beyond a maze of ridge crests. But from their moating glens they soar in ice-bound splendour, dazzle their pristine snows and impose their character upon your dreams; once seen, never to be forgotten.

But though the mountains invade your dreams, it will surely be the smiles of the people living among them that demand a return. A cry of "Namaste" hangs in the air. "Come as a tourist, but go as a friend" is their request - and who can resist?

Trekking routes described in these pages will reveal scenes of great beauty; scenes of forest, gorge and glacial glory, of deep valley and crenellated peak, of river and lake and waterfall. There'll be houses clustered like swallows' nests on steep-plunging ridge-crests, and hillsides terraced with rice, maize, buckwheat and millet. There'll be lofty rhododendron trees blazing scarlet in spring, edelweiss and gentian starring the scant pastures of autumn. Overhead lammergeier float effortlessly in the thermals and cast their great cross-shadows on the frozen earth. White-faced monkeys spook the forests, yaks lumber on dust-laden trails, tethered buffalo belch beneath a bamboo awning. And people; always people, for this is no blank mountain wilderness. Villagers, farmers, porters and children punctuate the hours of travel and add to the trekker's experience.

How you interact with the inhabitants of this enchanted land will depend on your sensitivity. Forget delusions of grandeur. Cast aside any preconceived notion that the ways of the West are necessarily better than those of Nepal. Here are people whose culture, background, faith and outlook have developed in different ways and at a different pace to our own. Grow receptive to their ways. Look, listen and learn and you'll come away enriched.

The mountains of the Himalaya may crowd your dreams. Let the people who live in their shadow invade your soul.

Trekking the trails of Nepal under normal conditions is neither more nor less potentially dangerous than walking among mountains anywhere. It's a physically demanding exercise where caution is often required, and a degree of stamina essential in order to gain the most from it. Most trekkers acknowledge this, but still there are those who go to the Himalaya without any previous mountain walking experience, preparation, or realisation of what trekking entails. Dangers do exist, and every year accidents happen. Trekkers die of hypothermia, of acute mountain sickness. Or they simply fall from the trail. All who wander there should remain alert, be vigilant to the possibility of landslip, stonefall, crumbling paths and greasy rocks. And remember, Nepal has no organised mountain rescue service of the kind in operation among certain mountain ranges of the West. If an accident happens self-help may be the only option.

Anyone following routes described in this book should assume responsibility for their own safety, and look to the needs of those with them.

Trail information outlined in the following pages reflects as accurately as possible routes experienced during research. However, readers should bear in mind that each monsoon adds its own signature to the landscape. Paths and bridges may be washed away and replaced elsewhere; villages expand, tea-houses and lodges multiply, and trails are often re-routed as a result of landslips reshaping a hillside. In order to improve and update future editions of this guide I'd appreciate the assistance of readers who could provide a note of changes found on trek. I would also welcome any comments or suggestions that might benefit trekkers in the future. All notes and corrections sent to me via the publisher will be gratefully received.

Please bear in mind that heights and distances quoted may not be entirely accurate. Different maps give varying figures and widely disparate spellings for some of the villages, mountains and passes. None of this should matter too much, though, for most of the names at least should be fairly obvious.

Basic sketch maps are provided to help with general orientation, route profiles to give an idea of the ups and downs of each trek day by day. Details of conventional map sheets, where they exist, are given in the Introduction, but even the best of these contain inaccuracies. In general trekkers in Langtang, Gosainkund and

Helambu need only refer to maps to ascertain the name of the next village or neighbouring mountain. Route-finding, for those travelling independently without a guide, is often achieved by word of mouth. Know the name of the next village on your route, and simply ask directions of a local Nepali. That is how Nepalis themselves find their way in unfamiliar country.

Times given for the various stages on trek are estimates only, but are offered as a rough indication of how long it's likely to take to walk from village to village. They do not allow for tea-house delays, nor photographic interruptions - and there'll be plenty of these - but are based on actual walking time. Whilst I have made attempts at consistency, variations are bound to have crept in over the course of several weeks on trek. My advice is to use these times as a rough guide, not as a challenge.

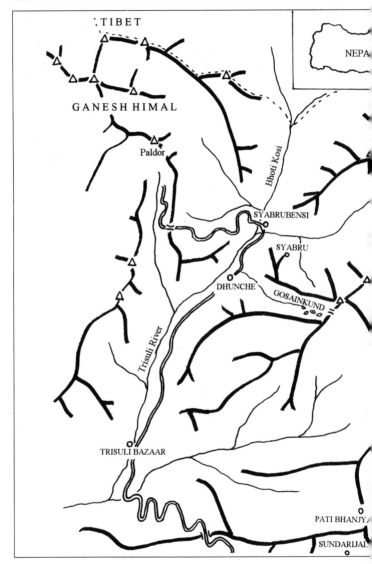

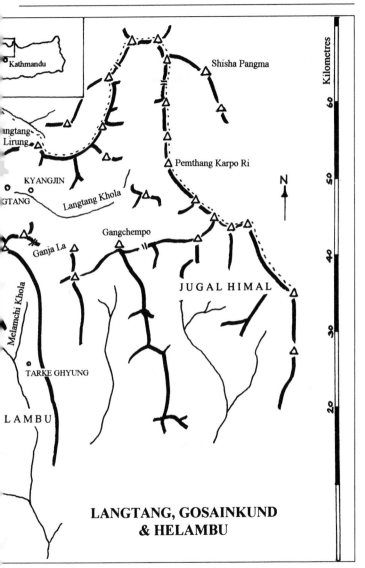

Kathmandu

Shisha Pangma

Langtang
Lirung

Pemthang Karpo Ri

KYANGJIN

GTANG

Langtang Khola

N

Ganja La

Gangchempo

JUGAL HIMAL

Melamchi Khola

TARKE GHYUNG

LAMBU

**LANGTANG, GOSAINKUND
& HELAMBU**

Kilometres

60

50

40

30

20

Introduction

*In a hundred ages of the gods I could not tell thee of the
glories of the Himalaya.* (Skanda Purana)

North of Kathmandu, beyond the rim of the valley and seen from city
rooftops, white crests of snow challenge the distant clouds. Get high
enough - one of the nearby modest hills will suffice - and an impressive
horizon beckons. There, rank upon rank of crystal mountains stand
sharp against the sky and hold the dying sun long after the valley has
given in to darkness: peaks of the Ganesh Himal, of Langtang, Jugal
and Rolwaling butt one against another, shoulder to shoulder as far
as the eye can see until sky pulls shutters tight onto the earth.

Divided from the Ganesh peaks by the deep trench of the Trisuli
Valley, the Langtang Himal is a block of attractive, shapely mountains
whose northern flanks sweep down into Tibet, and whose southern
side is attended by several minor peaks reached by non-technical
routes that provide stunning views of larger game, as well as the
splendours of the valley below. That valley, the valley of the Langtang
Khola, drains roughly east to west before emptying into the Trisuli
below Syabrubensi. It's a valley full of charm; stark and
uncompromising at its head, a classic glaciated U-shaped glen in its
middle sections, a narrow forested gorge in its lower reaches. At its
upper, eastern, end there's a wild outlook of soaring snow-and-ice-
capped mountains rimmed with glaciers bordered in the south by the
small but elegant Jugal Himal, while the main southern wall is lined
with mountains that effectively block out Helambu.

With plenty of lodges between Dhunche and Kyangjin (at 3749m:
12,300ft the highest accommodation in the valley), and by virtue of a
road-link with Kathmandu, trekking Langtang is possible in a round-
trip of as little as a week, to and from the roadhead. But trekkers do
themselves, and the valley, a disservice by rushing it. There is so
much to see and to do there, with glaciers to visit, minor summits to
wander up, and views to enjoy, that two full weeks could happily be
spent exploring. Route descriptions and ideas for further exploration

are given in the main body of this book, together with options for linking the Langtang Valley with Gosainkund and Helambu via a choice of passes.

Between Kathmandu's valley and the snowpeaks of Langtang, and providing a direct contrast to its higher, neighbouring region, Helambu offers a series of parallel foothill ridges separated by deep river valleys. These ridges push north to south; forested here, scarred with erosion there, rucked and wrinkled and terraced with immaculate precision, skill and dogged hard labour over countless generations by people who call themselves Sherpas, although in custom, dress and language they are very different to the better-known Sherpas of Solu-Khumbu. Helambu may not give an opportunity for trekkers to make close acquaintance with dramatic peaks of the Himalayan divide, but views north from the foothill crests reward with an incredible line of snow mountains that contrast in a most charming way with the luxuriant vegetation of Helambu itself.

This is the closest trekking region to Kathmandu. An hour's bus ride from the capital puts you in touch with a trail that climbs out of Sundarijal, and from the crest of the ridge above, all of Helambu is spread out in patterns of artistry ahead, backed by an immense skyline of countless chiselled peaks. A trekking circuit of seven or eight days gives a fine introduction to this foothill country, but no-one should assume that because altitudes are modest by Himalayan standards (Tharepati is the highest point at 3490m: 11,450ft) trekking here is without its demands, for there are some extremely long and steep uphill sections that are more severe than anything on the basic Langtang trek. As Tilman once said of a trail not far from here: "Its course resembled the line traced on a barograph in very unsettled weather." Lodges will be found in most, if not all, villages. Standards of accommodation are generally not as high as on offer at some of the lodges in the Annapurna and Everest regions, but should be perfectly acceptable to anyone with experience of mountain huts in the Western Alps of Europe.

South-west of the Langtang Valley, and north-west of Helambu, rises the Gosainkund Lekh, a mountain wall varying in altitude from 3000 to 5000 metres (9800-16,400ft). Caught within its upper folds and basins lie numerous small lakes, one of the largest being Gosainkunda, site of a major Hindu festival which attracts thousands of pilgrims during the full moon of July-August. A clutch of rather basic lodges will be found on the north shore of this lake.

Whilst Gosainkund may be approached directly from Dhunche, most trekkers add a visit there to an exploration of either Langtang or Helambu, for the Laurebina La (4610m: 15,125ft) just above the lakes makes an obvious route of passage from one region to the other, although in certain conditions it can prove difficult when approached from Helambu. In the wake of fresh snowfall the pass can be dangerous and should be avoided by inexperienced trekkers.

*

After the Annapurna and Everest regions the Langtang National Park, which covers all the area included in this guide, provides the best opportunities for independent trekking in all Nepal. There are plenty of lodges and group camping areas throughout, trails are mostly clear, and altitudes less severe than experienced on many other Himalayan destinations. Visual and cultural rewards are outstanding, and although the mountains that form a daily background to these treks may not provoke an instant spark of recognition, their beauty is undisputed. Langtang Lirung, Gangchenpo, Langshisa Ri, Pemthang Karpo Ri, Dorje Lakpa...their names may mean nothing before you go, but these are no second division peaks; gaze on them once and their architecture becomes ingrained on your memory.

Langtang National Park was established in 1976. With an area of 1710 square kilometres (660 sq miles) it is Nepal's second largest after Shey-Phoksumdo in Dolpo. Extending over the Langtang Valley, upper Helambu, Gosainkund Lekh and the Jugal Himal east of Helambu, the Park contains habitats ranging from sub-tropical to alpine. Extravagant displays of rhododendron in spring provide just one obvious appeal, but in addition the Park boasts around 1000 plant species, 160 birds and 30 species of mammal, including Himalayan tahr, musk deer and the lesser panda.

All this creates the background to some of the most rewarding treks in all Nepal.

TREKKING AND TREKKING STYLES

There are many ways to enjoy mountains: some persons engage their passion by cutting steps into impossible ice walls, others entrust their lives to one fragile piton in a rocky crevice, and still others, I among them, prefer simply to roam the high country.
(George B.Schaller)

To "simply to roam the high country" is a perfect summary of what trekking is all about.

Trekking is, of course, the simplest way to travel - on foot. While the modern world-traveller is often dependent on third-party schedules and the vagaries of mechanical aid, the trekker in Nepal opts for destinations where wheeled transport is unknown, and where walking is the only way to get from A to B - on routes that have been in existence, in many cases, for hundreds of years. Trade routes, farmers' routes, hunters' trails, paths made by yaks heading for pasture. Long ribbons of trails wind up and down the hills, scrape along steep cliffs, cross high passes, explore remote glens, visit pilgrim sites, link villages and valleys, and almost always reward with some of the loveliest views imaginable. Whilst trekking one is tempted to echo Robert Louis Stevenson's oft-quoted maxim: "To travel hopefully is a better thing than to arrive, and the true success is to labour." Labour is part of it, and you need to be fit.

Trekking is to journey through an unfamiliar land, moving on day after day as though on pilgrimage. And in common with the pilgrim those who gain most from it are those who have managed to cast off the anxieties that beset their everyday life, who can ignore daily inconveniences, and instead readily absorb each new experience that arises and live in every moment of the present.

Wandering the trails of Langtang, Gosainkund or Helambu can be, and should be, a life-enriching experience. Since the rate of progress through each day is self-governing, opportunities abound for observing the intricacies of the route, of the life of the countryside through which the trails lead, the villages, forests and ridge crests, the trees and shrubs, animals, birds and butterflies, the ever-changing light on a distant mountain, the thunder of a glacier-charged river,

15

tinkle of a yak bell, the slap of a prayer flag in the wind, the welcoming call of *Namaste*. There are scents, too, to draw upon. In the foothills they may be heavy with sun-drenched vegetation, while at altitude the crisp fragrance of morning is a tonic that sharpens every sense. There's the taste of dust, the smell of woodsmoke, the acrid, eye-smarting effects of a yak-dung fire in a simple lodge.

In common with most trekking regions in Nepal Langtang and Helambu do not offer a true wilderness experience, for there are villages or hamlets scattered along the greater part of the trails described in these treks. Upvalley beyond the final lodges at Kyangjin there are a few groups of yak herders' huts, and you'd need to delve more than a day's walk from Kyangjin, and carry camping gear and food, before the Langtang Valley shows little sign of man's influence. Helambu is even more heavily settled, while Gosainkund has its collection of trekkers' lodges.

The tourist infrastructure that has developed along these trails enables a choice of trekking styles to be enjoyed. These may be summarised as follows: trekking with a group under the auspices of a commercial agency (adventure travel company); independent trekking - sometimes referred to as tea-house trekking; and a third option, which is a cross between group travel and independent trekking, and which entails hiring a porter-guide to carry the trekker's gear and to lead him along the trail using lodges for overnight accommodation.

The choice of style to suit you will depend upon many considerations such as cost, personal experience, availability of friends to trek with, amount of time required to organise and carry out the trek, which route to follow, etc. The following paragraphs, therefore, discuss options available in some detail, with specific regard to the Langtang, Gosainkund and Helambu regions.

Trekking with an Adventure Travel Company:

Group trekking in Nepal developed from the tried and tested method of approach set by decades of Himalayan expeditions on the way to their chosen mountain. Trekkers sleep in tents, are catered for by trained cooks and kitchen boys, and are cosseted by a staff of sherpas (as far as trekking is concerned a sherpa is a member of the trek crew, who may or may not be a true Sherpa). They are led by a local guide, and have the main burden of equipment carried by an army of porters - the whole expedition overseen by a sirdar (chief guide) who usually speaks some English, and in many cases accompanied by an experienced Western leader.

This is the obvious choice for those with more money than time at their disposal, who dislike the hassles of organisation, who get frustrated with bureaucracy, or who have limited mountain experience and want a degree of security. Trekking with a reputable adventure travel company does away with all pre-departure worries and trek concerns, thus enabling the trekker to enjoy the experience unfussed by detail upon arrival in Nepal. Read the brochures and all dossiers carefully, sign the form, make out your cheque and let someone else take care of the arrangements. One of the most important things you are paying for is expertise.

A product of this expertise is pre-departure advice with regard to innoculations, visa requirements and a suggested kit list. All flights to and from Kathmandu, and transfers and other travel arrangements within Nepal, will normally be taken care of, as will hotel accommodation and the provision of trekking permits. Some companies also make available for hire certain items of equipment that would otherwise be rather expensive for the first-time trekker to buy, like a good-quality sleeping bag or a duvet suitable for wear at high altitudes.

On a group trek porters carry all camping equipment, food, kitchen stores and personal baggage, leaving the trekker free to shoulder little more than a light rucksack containing a few items likely to be required during the day, such as water bottle, camera, spare film, pullover or duvet.

Nights are almost always spent in tents. Meals are prepared and served by a staff of Nepalese cooks and kitchen boys who will have undergone some training in hygiene requirements and who understand the types of food favoured by Western trekkers. Latrines are dug by the trek crew, tents erected and dismantled for you, and guides ensure you do not get lost along the trail. Whilst the sirdar carries overall responsibility for choice of campsite, the hire and fire of porters and decisions with regard to choice of route and whether it is safe to attempt the crossing of a high pass, the Western leader, where employed, acts as a liaison between the group and the local staff. He or she will often have an understanding of any medical problems likely to be encountered, and is in charge of a comprehensive first aid kit. Some U.K. based companies offer financial incentives to qualified medical personnel who accompany groups on particularly remote treks, but this is not likely to apply to routes featured in this book.

Trekking with a group is a very sociable way to travel. Daily you will be walking, and sharing experiences, with people whom you may never have met before, and lasting relationships often develop from on-trek introductions. The downside is that on occasion you may find it difficult to get on with another member of the group, in which case a degree of tact may need to be exercised in order to avoid a clash of personalities. On the whole groups tend to be of sufficient size (10-14 is normal) to make it possible to steer clear of anyone whose personality rubs against your own, without it becoming too obvious. Friction on an organised trek is rare, and when it does occur it is usually short-lived.

On group treks there is an unfortunate, but understandable, tendency to carry your own culture with you, to mix only with fellow members both along the trail and in camp, thereby missing opportunities to make contact with local people.

Organised parties, of course, generally need to keep to a predetermined route and maintain a fairly tight schedule, which can be a little frustrating if you pass an enticing side glen you'd like to visit. On the other hand, since each day's stage is limited by the distance a porter carrying a 30kg (66lbs) load can cover, the journey is made at a leisurely pace, thus allowing plenty of time to enjoy the scenery, visit an occasional monastery, study the flowers or indulge in an orgy of photography along the trail.

There is a routine to the group trekker's day which usually begins with a mug of tea being thrust through the tent flap at around 6am, closely followed by a bowl of warm water for washing. Breakfast is served soon after. This is generally a filling meal that includes porridge or muesli, eggs and chapatis, tea, coffee or hot chocolate. In the foothills this will be eaten outdoors with views of distant mountains and hills warming to the new day. At higher, colder, altitudes a mess tent will be used.

The day's walk starts early, at around 7.30am when the light is pure, the air cool and birds active. The trek crew breaks camp as the porters pack their *dokos* (large conical baskets in which goods are carried) and set off along the trail. Porters walk at their own pace, stop for frequent rests at *chautaaras* and cook their own food over small trailside fires along the way. Beware that you may not see the porter again who is carrying your own personal baggage until long after you reach the next camp, so make sure you have with you anything you may need during the day. During the morning's walk the kitchen crew will rattle past and select a lunch spot, often with a fine view. Lunch is eaten any time between 11am and 1pm. This is often a hot meal with plenty of liquids.

The afternoon's walk will normally end before 4pm, giving the chance to write journal notes, read or chat with other members of the group while camp is being set up and the evening meal prepared - another three-course meal that is usually finished by 6.30 or 7pm, allowing plenty of time to rest, read, talk or listen to the songs of the sherpas beneath a starlit sky. In my experience it's not unusual for members of a group trek to be in their sleeping bags soon after 8pm!

One of the positive aspects of trekking with a commercial group is that with a trained cook and kitchen staff as part of the crew, the standard of hygiene in the preparation of food can be controlled. This is an important matter over which independent tea-house trekkers have little influence in the lodges. A skilled Nepali cook will often provide a surprising variety of meals using just basic portable equipment, and is rightly seen in the trek crew hierarchy as number two after the sirdar. All groups trekking in the Langtang National Park must cook on kerosene or gas, although most lodges continue to burn wood or yak-dung on their cooking fires.

Adventure travel companies regularly advertise in the outdoor press, and a number of these organise promotional slide shows during the winter months, providing an ideal opportunity for potential clients to meet and question trek leaders and assess what's on offer. A list of UK based companies who promote treks in the Langtang and Helambu regions is given in Appendix B.

Independent Trekking:

For experienced travellers who either enjoy, or are not averse to making all arrangements - such as organising visas, booking flights, seeking accommodation in Kathmandu, queuing for permits, buying bus tickets to Dhumre or Sundarijal, route-finding on trek, choosing meals and lodges - independent tea-house trekking is the answer. It can be extremely rewarding, as well as being by far the cheapest method of trekking in Nepal, but to be successful it is essential to adopt a flexible attitude of mind and be ready to adapt to a variety of situations. The only predictable element of travel in a country like Nepal is the certainty that the unpredictable will happen!

Tea-house trekking is understandably popular in the Langtang National Park. Lodges here are numerous and on the whole are of a fairly high standard for Nepal, although there are still a number of very basic lodgings in such places as Changtang in the Langtang Valley, at Laurebinayak and Gosainkund, and at Phedi, Ghopte, Tharepati and a few small villages in Helambu.

It should be noted, however, that tea-house trekkers do not actually stay in tea-houses. As far as this guidebook is concerned, a tea-house is a trailside building that offers basic refreshment for travellers, while a lodge is a simple hotel (*bhatti*) where both food and shelter are provided. These *bhatti* are variously advertised as guest-houses, hotels, inns or lodges, but whatever the sign says outside, standards of accommodation are fairly basic by comparison with Western hotels - although it is inevitable that some places will provide a greater degree of comfort and service than others. It should also be borne in mind that the provision of accommodation for trekkers is undergoing constant change and improvement.

The following notes have been put together as a result of considerable experience of using lodges in assorted areas of Nepal, including the regions covered by this guidebook. I've tried to portray them as they are, both good and bad sides, without prejudice. Being aware of what's in store may help newcomers to this style of trekking. Remember, lodges provide a service that enables independent travellers to gain access to some magnificent country, and in themselves can be an important and memorable part of your trek. Go with a positive outlook and you'll enjoy each lodge you stay in.

Most lodges, or *bhatti*, consist of a simple building comprising kitchen, dining area and sleeping quarters. The majority have dormitory accommodation, but many also offer twin-bedded rooms. In a number of cases, particularly in Langtang, bedrooms are housed in a separate building to that of the kitchen/dining area. Dormitories may sleep as many as twenty trekkers, but are usually more spacious than some mountain huts in the European Alps. Twin-bedded rooms are little more than a small bare 'cell' furnished with two firm but perfectly adequate beds, each of which has a thin foam-rubber mattress and a pillow. Blankets and linen are not usually supplied, although it may sometimes be possible to rent a blanket if your sleeping bag is inadequate for the conditions. An insulation mat (Karrimat or similar) is recommended for additional comfort and as a barrier against possible infestation from some of the mattresses provided. There will be no floor covering, and the walls are generally little more than thin wooden planks that offer no sound-proofing at all (the romantically-inclined should take note!), and very rarely will there be even a hook from which to hang a few items of clothing or a towel. It's worth carrying a length of string and a couple of small screw-hooks to make your own portable clothes-line. Bedrooms, as opposed to dormitories, are usually secured with a padlock provided by the lodge owner.

Experienced tea-house trekkers quickly note the position of the kitchen fire and request a bed in a room well away from the possibility of escaping smoke. In those lodges where sleeping quarters are in a separate building, smoke will be no problem. Lack of heat may.

Washing facilities, where they exist, are primitive and sometimes consist of no more than a hosepipe outdoors. However, most lodge owners will happily provide a small bowl of warm water in which to wash. A few lodges advertise hot showers, but if you imagine a neat, tiled cubicle and abundant hot water - forget it. These 'showers' are often contained in a grubby outside shed where you luxuriate beneath a dribble of luke-warm water. Just occasionally you may be surprised, but don't bank on it. As most water is heated by dwindling stocks of firewood, you should seriously consider limiting the demand for showers to those lodges using solar-heating - and in these the water is sometimes actually hot.

Toilets (*charpi*) usually consist of a simple outbuilding with a hole in the floor over a pit. Few have water available for flushing; a number of them have a box or basket provided in which used toilet paper should be deposited, for burning later by the lodge owner. This may strike you at first as being pretty objectionable, but it's preferable

21

to the discarded clusters of pink toilet paper that litter some sections of trail. Use the toilets provided, and avoid treating the countryside as an open-air latrine. There's still a long way to go, admittedly, but standards of sanitation are slowly improving.

Dining rooms are often poorly lit, but in the best of them a convivial atmosphere is easily created. Since the hill people of Nepal have little concept of privacy, none should be expected. The children of lodge owners will often join you at table, pick up your books or camera, study your clothes and anything else left lying around. If you find this curiosity annoying, don't provide temptation, set firm limits but avoid losing your temper. This is their home, their country, and you are the guest who walked through an open door.

Bhatti owners offer a surprising choice of meals, although anyone who has trekked the trails of Annapurna or Everest will realise that Langtang and Helambu menus are not quite as ambitious as in those other popular areas. However, first-time trekkers who arrive expecting to exist on a diet of *daal bhat* three times a day will be pleasantly surprised by the range of foods on offer. Most of the time it will be possible to vary your diet between Western fare and local food, but it is important to remember that lodge meals are invariably cooked over a single fire, so it follows that if several trekkers order a variety of meals you can find yourself waiting a very long time (as much as two hours even) before being served. This can prove irksome, especially if you're hungry after a long day's trekking, but it also means that an unnecessary amount of firewood is being consumed. The trick is to assess what your fellow trekkers are ordering, and follow their lead. Some lodges have a few luxury items for sale: bottled drinks are found almost everywhere, while less frequently you may be able to buy biscuits, chocolate and sometimes tinned fruit and meats.

Whilst you're unlikely to have any control over hygiene in the lodge kitchen, a few common-sense precautions will help minimise the risk of stomach upsets: always wash your hands before meals, make sure the crockery and cutlery provided is both clean and dry, and exercise caution in your choice of food and drinks.

The standard procedure on arrival at a lodge is to enquire of the owner if there are any vacant beds. If so, claim yours as early as possible. If you'll be staying in a dormitory, lay out your sleeping bag on the chosen bed; if you're using a bedroom deposit your gear inside and ask for a padlock. It's a good idea to place your torch where you can locate it easily once darkness falls, as few lodges have any means of lighting other than candles. Find out what and where the washing and toilet facilities are, and if there's a set time by which meals should be ordered. Keep a note of all food and drinks consumed. Some lodges have a notebook in which to write your orders, in others the lodge owner keeps a note, while in a few it's left to the trekker to remember what has been taken. Prices are exceedingly modest by Western standards, and the cost of accommodation so low that the lodge keeper relies on the sale of meals and drinks to make a reasonable living. Do not book a bed in one lodge and eat elsewhere. Nor should you haggle over prices, no matter what may be the expectation in Kathmandu. Prices are usually set by the local community and will be standardised in any given village, so 'shopping around' for the most favourable price does not work here. Remember, however, that the farther you trek from a roadhead, the higher prices will be.

Independent trekkers are able to enjoy a much more flexible routine than those on an organised trek, and can vary their route at will. Although there is a danger of mixing only with fellow Westerners with whom they share the lodges, those who wish to learn more about local people, customs and the life of villages along the route will find that opportunities abound. However, the best way to enjoy cultural interaction is with the third method of trekking - in the company of a porter-guide.

Trekking with a Porter-Guide:

This is the answer for individuals who have no-one else to trek with, and for whom group trekking, for one reason or another, is ruled out. Trekking alone is not recommended, and although it is quite possible to find another Westerner willing to share the trails with you, the hiring of a porter-guide can be the key to a whole new world of experience.

A good porter-guide will become your trusty friend and companion who will provide a daily insight into the ways of the people whose country you're travelling through; as a consequence the opportunity for regular cultural exchange can be a highlight of

23

your trek. A porter-guide will carry some of your gear, make sure you keep on the correct trail and act as a link between yourself and locals met on the path. He may suggest alternative trails, less-trekked paths, and take you to sites of interest or local festivals as and when they occur well off the normal route of most other trekkers. A good porter-guide can teach you much of value and, if you're sensitive, eager to learn and prepared to treat your companion as a friend rather than a servant, your experience will be the more profound as a result.

There are, of course, plenty of people looking for work in Kathmandu, and many who claim to be guides. A guide, however, will not expect to carry a load for you, but will arrange to hire a porter to do just that, immediately adding to your expense. There's nothing wrong with that, but if you are happy to carry some of your own gear you should be able to manage very well with just one man to do the dual role of guiding and portering; hence the porter-guide.

How to choose such a man, however, is not easy; it can be very difficult to judge a person's reliability and trustworthiness in a short interview and, it has to be said, there are plenty of 'wide boys' offering their services on the streets of Kathmandu. Whilst a good porter-guide can make your trek a daily delight, a bad one will give plenty of cause for regret. Perhaps the safest and most sensible way, then, is to hire a man through one of the local trekking agencies, such as Mt Kailash Paradise Trekking see Appendix B), who will also arrange his insurance - a legal requirement.

In such well-trekked areas as Langtang, Gosainkund and Helambu, it's not essential to have a guide simply to keep you on the correct trail - although there are many instances of trekkers getting lost even here. But on occasion you may feel the need to have someone carry your rucksack for you. In this case a porter is all that you need, and it's often possible to hire one along the route at short notice - either for just a day or two, or for the duration of your trek. Enquire of your lodge owner for a reputable local - preferably one who speaks a few words of English. Payment is normally based on a set fee per day, inclusive of food and lodging, or a higher wage with the requirement that he provides his own food. The latter is usually the preferred option. It is worth remembering that the role of a porter is by no means a demeaning one, for portering has long formed a major source of employment throughout the hill regions of Nepal.

Once you hire a man you assume employer's responsibility for his well-being. This is true of a porter-guide as for a porter. You should make sure that he is adequately clothed and equipped to cope with below-freezing temperatures in the event of your proposed route involving the crossing of a high pass (the Laurebina La, or Ganja La for example), or if you're trekking in winter. While a porter-guide hired through a Kathmandu agency may be expected to be well-equipped, one hired 'off the street' or from a lowland village might have little idea of conditions higher in the mountains, in which case it is up to you to provide him with warm clothing once you get high. And there's little opportunity to buy such gear once you leave Kathmandu.

Organising your own trek:

It may be that you have a group of friends with whom you'd like to go trekking in Langtang and/or Helambu and you fancy exploring more remote regions off the beaten track - perhaps straying into the neighbouring Jugal Himal, for example, or planning to cross the Ganja La where for several days there are no lodges. In such cases you will need tents and food, and unless you're prepared to backpack a heavy load, this will involve hiring porters and, possibly, cooks and guides as well. It's quite possible that one of the mainstream UK trekking companies would be prepared to organise such a mini-expedition for you. Bufo Ventures specialise in arranging trips for independent trekkers, so it may be worth getting in touch to see if they can help. (See Appendix B.)

Alternatively, you can work directly with one of the Kathmandu agencies also listed in the Appendix. Either contact them in advance, or when you arrive in Nepal. In the latter case they'll probably need four or five days' warning before you intend to set out. They will hire the necessary manpower on your behalf, provide tents, cooking equipment and also food, and arrange permits for you.

Solo trekking - a word of warning:

For safety purposes trekking alone is not recommended. If you'd rather not travel in an organised group, have no friend available to trek with you, and prefer not to hire a porter-guide, it's possible to advertise for a companion in Kathmandu at the office of the Himalayan

Rescue Association, which is situated almost next door to the Central Immigration Office. A number of solo travellers advertise in this way and you may be lucky. Alternatively, pin a request on the notice board of your hotel.

TREKKING LANGTANG, GOSAINKUND AND HELAMBU

Tread softly, for this is holy ground./It may be, could we look with seeing eyes,/This spot we stand upon is paradise.
(Christina Rossetti)

Holy ground? The Langtang Valley has long been a special place for Buddhists, and the high lake of Gosainkunda is sacred to Hindus. As for Helambu, stand on one of the rhododendron-bound ridge crests and gaze north and it may be, with seeing eyes, you too will find your own version of paradise.

Whether you have a week, ten days, a fortnight or a month to spend on trek, trails described in this book will provide plenty of ideas to fill your time and give a wealth of memorable experiences. The following brief outlines give an overview of possibilities, while more detail is provided in the main body of the book.

Langtang:

Dhunche to Kyangjin and Langshisa Kharka: (4-5 days up; 3-4 days down)
This is a splendid there-and-back trek of only moderate difficulty, of equal value to tea-house trekkers as to those travelling with a group and sleeping in tents. Additional days should be allowed, where possible, in order to explore the upper part of the valley and to wander to the summit of one or more of the small peaks above Kyangjin Gompa that provide spectacular viewpoints.

Dhunche is a bustling village on the left (east) bank of the Trisuli Valley, and is accessible by road from Kathmandu. Although it is only 112 kilometres (70 miles) from the capital the road is dreadful, and the journey by bus will take all day. Sometimes the road between Trisuli Bazaar and Dhunche is cut by landslip during the monsoon rains. At such times passengers have to transfer to another bus or truck waiting (hopefully) on the far side. It all makes for interesting travel.

From Dhunche the trail crosses spurs of hillside to Syabru before entering the lower forested region of the Langtang Valley proper. In its lower reaches the valley is a narrow, steep-sided gorge, and views of the mountains are severely restricted until shortly before coming out of forest near Ghora Tabela, a long day's walk from Syabru.

On the approach to Langtang village the valley begins to open out and snow-capped mountains tease ahead in the east where big peaks border the Jugal Himal. Langtang Lirung which soars above the village is not seen to full effect until much later, but after leaving Langtang on the stage which leads to Kyangjin the high mountain scenery is quite stunning. You may possibly begin to feel the effects of altitude on this stage, in which case caution is advised.

Kyangjin, or Kyangjin Gompa (3749m: 12,300ft) as the collection of lodges has become known, offers the highest available accommodation here, but campers could continue upvalley for a further day to wild country below and beyond the handsome peak of Gangchempo. There are several yak pastures that would make idyllic campsites. Langshisa Kharka (4084m: 13,399ft) is a solitary stone hut set in rough pasture near converging glaciers and is about as far as most trekkers would be prepared to go. The walk to it from Kyangjin is, quite simply, magnificent.

The return could be varied by remaining on the right bank of the Langtang Khola all the way to Syabrubensi, a village at the junction of the Langtang and Trisuli valleys, then follow the dirt road back to Dhunche.

Alternative ways out of the Langtang Valley are given below.

Langtang to Gosainkund: (4 days)

Probably the most popular way of extending a trek in the Langtang Valley is to visit the lakes of Gosainkund. The best and easiest trail leads from Syabru, so it is necessary to backtrack from Langtang to this fine hillcrest village (two days from Kyangjin Gompa), then climb steep hillsides via Sing Gompa and Laurebinayak to the lodges at Gosainkund. Allow two days from Syabru. Gosainkund then provides an opportunity to return to Kathmandu via either Helambu

(4-5 days), or by descending directly to Dhunche (1 day) for the bus out.

Langtang to Helambu via the Ganja La: (4-5 days + 3-4 days in Helambu)
The Ganja La (5200m: 17,060ft) is a high pass on the south side of the Langtang Valley, accessible from Kyangjin Gompa, that makes an obvious linking route to the village of Tarke Ghyang in Helambu. However, the pass can be tricky, especially in snowy conditions, when mountaineering experience will be required to make a safe crossing. It is normally possible between May and November, but even in the best of conditions a tent, plus food and cooking fuel for about four or five days, should be carried. You will need a guide too, as it is easy to lose the way when faced with limited visibility.

Langtang to the Jugal Himal via Tilman's Pass: (9-10 days)
This third option is for experienced mountaineers only as the pass (5304m: 17,402ft) can be both difficult and dangerous. Only a group that is fully equipped with porters, tents, food and fuel for about 9-10 days from Kyangjin, should consider this route. The pass, crossed by Tilman in 1949, lies above a tributary of the Langshisa Glacier, between the peaks of Gangchempo and Urkinmang, and leads into the head of a valley system draining the Jugal Himal. There are no lodges in Jugal.

Gosainkund:

Dhunche to Gosainkund (2-3 days up; 1-2 days down)
There are two ways to reach Gosainkund from Dhunche, both trails converging at Sing Gompa. The direct route climbs steeply away from the dirt road between Dhunche and Bharkhu, goes through forest of fir and rhododendron and emerges near the cheese factory at Sing Gompa. The alternative will take an extra day (three days in all), and goes via Syabru to join the route suggested from Langtang. From Sing Gompa the trail rises along an open crest with an immense panorama to enjoy all the way to the rough lodges at Laurebinayak, about halfway between Sing Gompa and Gosainkund. The route is clear, given reasonable conditions, but quite steep in places. There are plenty of tea-houses and sufficient lodges to make camping superfluous.

Sundarijal to Gosainkund: (5-6 days up; 4-5 days down)

Easily reached by public bus from Kathmandu in about an hour, Sundarijal is an ideal starting place for treks through Helambu and up to Gosainkund. The standard route from here is fairly strenuous, with plenty of height gain on some stages. Lodges are plentiful, but they become very basic in the upper section of the trek - from Kutumsang on. A number of organised groups choose this route, but camping can be a little rough beyond Tharepati. Views are quite spectacular between Chisapani and Kutumsang, and again from the Laurebina La just above Gosainkund. A splendid trek.

Alternative routes from Gosainkund are outlined below.

Gosainkund to Dhunche: (1-2 days)

The shortest return route to Kathmandu from Gosainkund is by direct descent to Dhunche in the Trisuli Valley (1-2 days), and by bus from there. A more pleasant option is to descend to Dhunche by way of Syabru (2 days).

Gosainkund to Langtang: (5 days + options)

An obvious continuation of the trek is to descend to Syabru via Sing Gompa, and there join the main Langtang route outlined above. This would need about five days to reach Kyangjin, and another 3-4 days to return to Dhunche for the bus ride back to Kathmandu. Allow 15-16 days in all - Sundarijal to Dhunche via Gosainkund and the Langtang Valley - plus extra days for exploring above Kyangjin. (See paragraph below headed Langtang-Gosainkund-Helambu.)

Helambu:

Sundarijal-Tharepati-Melamchigaon-Talamarang-Pati Bhanjyang-Sundarijal: (7-8 days)

The name Helambu (or Helmu) actually refers to the northern end of the Melamchi Khola valley, but is more generally accepted as being those ridge and valley systems that flow down to the rim of the Kathmandu Valley.

This is a fine clockwise circuit of the region that makes a good introduction to trekking in Nepal. Again, as there are lodges throughout, it would suit independent tea-house trekkers as well as organised groups. Being a circuit it could be tackled in either direction - the meeting point being Pati Bhanjyang early on day two, or late on the first stage - but the preferable way to travel is clockwise to make the most of the views, which are especially fine looking north from the ridge crests.

Leaving Sundarijal a long, wearisome climb leads to a wooded pass from which a short descent is made to the lodges of Chisapani. This is usually far enough for a first day, although some trekkers prefer to continue down to Pati Bhanjyang. From there a series of ridge crests on the western edge of Helambu will be followed for a further 2-3 days as far as the lodge village of Tharepati at 3490 metres (11,450ft). Here a trail drops eastward to Melamchigaon in the valley of the Melamchi Khola, then climbs to Tarke Ghyang on the eastern hillside high above the river. This river valley is then followed roughly southward to Talamarang and a junction of trails. The Helambu circuit is closed by bearing west with a climb to Pati Bhanjyang.

Langtang-Gosainkund-Helambu:

A magnificent trek, combining all three areas and starting either in Dhunche or Sundarijal, can be achieved in about two weeks. However, it would be worth adding some extra days for rest, acclimatisation and/or the opportunity to explore the upper reaches of the Langtang Valley. Such a combined expedition may be classed as one of the great treks of Nepal.

TREKKING SEASONS

Seasonal weather is rather less predictable than weather day by day. (H.W.Tilman)

If Tilman's *Nepal Himalaya* is the only book you read before visiting Langtang, you'd be forgiven for believing it rains all the time. Unfortunately, his first trip there coincided with the monsoon, so his views - both literal and metaphorical - were somewhat clouded. But it is true to say that if you don't mind leeches, mud, heat and torrential rain, trekking somewhere in Nepal is possible at any time of the year, including the monsoon. However, the main seasons for trekking are generally considered as being the spring, pre-monsoon period, and the post-monsoon months of October, November and early December. Between December and the spring, days and nights in Langtang and Gosainkund can be bitterly cold, but parts of Helambu may be trekked throughout the winter.

The post-monsoon period is the most popular among trekkers, and lodges and trails will then be at their busiest in the regions covered by this guide. The weather is generally settled, although a little light rain and the occasional flurry of snow may be encountered. Days are blessed with clear, often cloud-free skies, and the temperature very pleasant, although nights can feel quite cold above 3000 metres (9800ft) from mid-October on. In December and January night-time temperatures will almost certainly be below freezing at altitudes upwards of 3000 metres.

During mid-winter snow can effectively close trails over Tilman's Pass, the Ganja La and even the Laurebina La above Gosainkund which is often impassable from late November to March. Some of the lodges may also be closed, thus disrupting some trekking routes.

The spring trekking season runs from late February or March through to May. Rhododendrons come into flower at this time and beautiful displays are seen in parts of Helambu, and on the approach to Gosainkund from Sing Gompa. As spring progresses so the weather grows much warmer, bringing frequent storms and with haze or clouds often obscuring the views. By May temperatures can be quite oppressive below 3000 metres.

ENVIRONMENTAL CONSIDERATIONS

Yet each man kills the thing he loves. (Oscar Wilde)

Tourism brings financial benefits to some of the Nepalese hill-folk. It also brings problems. The negative effects of trekking have received much publicity in recent years, and are now widely recognised, although still there are newcomers to Nepal who remain unaware of their potential impact on what is, after all, a fragile environment. Before going on trek it is worth visiting the information centre of KEEP (Kathmandu Environmental Education Project) on Tridevi Marg, near Kathmandu's Central Immigration Office, or get hold of a copy of Wendy Brewer Lama's admirable booklet, *Trekking Gently in the Himalaya.*

Fuel-efficient trekking:

Without wishing to overstate the case, a need for environmental awareness on trek is essential in order to minimise the strain which each one of us puts on local resources. Firewood is an obvious example. National Park rules prohibit the burning of wood by trekkers, yet although group cooks will make use of kerosene-burning Primus stoves, porters carrying for those same groups continue to prepare their own food on firewood taken from the forests, while most of the lodges patronised by trekkers still use firewood for cooking and for heating water.

In those regions above the treeline where timber is scarce, dried yak dung is used as an alternative to firewood. You might imagine then that burning yak dung is okay - until you breathe in the smoke, that is. After all, this won't lead to deforestation. But by collecting dung for their cooking stoves, lodge owners are reducing the amount of fertiliser available for spreading on the fields. Crop reductions follow.

In order to help reduce the demand for cooking fuel of either variety, trekkers using lodges should avoid ordering complicated meals, but instead choose easy-to-cook foods and try to order these at the same time as other lodge users. It's also important to limit the demand for showers to those lodges where water is heated by solar panels, and rather than keep stoking a fire to keep warm in the evening, wear more or better clothes and go to bed early. Where possible organisers of group treks should make arrangements to either provide kerosene stoves for their porters, or to cook for them, and to outlaw the call for campfires.

Rubbish disposal:

Contrary to the statements of some pundits the problem of litter in the

Dhunche is an important little township at the start of the Langtang trek
Tibetan snowpeaks form a backdrop on the trail to Syabru

East of Thangsep views upvalley are partially restricted by mountain spurs
Bridge over the Langtang Khola below Kyangjin

Himalaya is not something that has only become apparent since the advent of trekking - although it has been exacerbated by increased numbers, of course. Before the war, a visitor to the Zemu Glacier on Kanchenjunga in 1938 found "the amount of rubbish strewn about was reminiscent of the day after a Bank Holiday at one of England's more popular beauty spots." That ill-disposed rubbish is not simply a recent phenomenon, nor one that is limited to a mountain environment, is no excuse. Litter should be unacceptable wherever and whenever it is found.

Nepalese villagers have no historic culture of litter disposal, for until the advent of plastics, tin and glass, there was no real problem. Any waste was biodegradable. But now locals, trekkers and mountaineering expeditions alike carry into the hills varying amounts of goods that at some stage will need to be disposed of; from plastic water containers to medical products and torch and camera batteries. It has been estimated that a group of 15 trekkers generates around 24kg (52lbs) of non-burnable, non-degradable rubbish in the course of a two-week trek. Add to that natural body waste, toilet and tissue paper, and the scale of the problem may be imagined.

Everyone can help by disposing of their own rubbish in a considerate manner. If you're trekking with a group your leader should arrange for all non-burnable waste to be collected in plastic bags and carried out. Independent trekkers should find space in their own rucksacks for carrying rubbish. Burnables should be gathered and destroyed in a common pit at the campsite, making sure that no papers are left to blow away or be dug up by animals. Never leave litter of any kind along the trail, but take it with you. Wendy Brewer Lama estimates that nearly a quarter of a million batteries are used by trekkers each year, but as there are no proper means for their disposal in Nepal, all used batteries should be taken home to be disposed of safely.

As for toilet demands, most lodges and tea-houses have a form of latrine that should be used when required, and group trekkers must be provided with a toilet tent too. These should be sited as least 50 metres (150ft) from water sources, the hole deep enough to meet the needs of the group and a square of turf kept to one side for replacing later. Burn your own toilet paper after use and sprinkle a little dirt in the hole to discourage flies, and make sure the toilet pit is properly

filled in and covered before leaving the campsite.

If you get caught out along the trail, as happens to most of us at some time or other, choose your site with care, dig a hole with a small trowel or penknife and fill it in afterwards. Don't forget to carefully burn used toilet paper too. (Keep a lighter or matches with your toilet roll for just such an occasion.)

Don't pollute the water:

Streams and rivers are often the only water source for villages in the hill regions of the Himalaya, so it is important to avoid polluting them. Do not bathe or wash clothes in them, nor be tempted to use soap or shampoo in any hot springs you come across. Washing and laundry can be achieved by use of a small bowl borrowed from a lodge or your trek crew if you're travelling with a group, the soapy residue being disposed of well away from a water source. Bring biodegradable soap from home.

CULTURAL INTERACTION

Nepal is there to change you, not for you to change Nepal.
(Oft-quoted maxim; origin unknown.)

When it comes to cross-cultural interaction, most of us are innocents abroad. Our Western society does little to prepare us for the kaleidoscopic cultures of the East, and it is sheer arrogance to assume that our ways are superior to those of 'simple' Nepali hill-folk. Their culture has developed separately from ours - which is one of the reasons why many of us choose to visit the Himalaya in the first place - and observation of its intricacies forms an important ingredient in successful trekking. If we wish to gain maximum benefit from the full trekking experience, we must observe all we can and learn from those observations. Then we may discover that our hosts have more to teach us in regard to living in contentment than we can possibly teach them. In the unfussed ways of villagers met on trek we learn that patience, kindness and tolerance for all are virtues worth striving for. In turn it is essential that we observe certain rules of behaviour in

order to avoid giving offence to our hosts. The following guidelines, once studied, should become second nature after a few days on the trail.

Affection: Avoid public displays of affection. Kissing, cuddling and even holding hands in public are frowned upon by local people.

Begging: In general, don't encourage it. Children who ask for school pens, balloons, money or sweets should be discouraged. Aiding children to become beggars will only erode their self-respect. On the other hand, donations to schools, health centres or other worthwhile projects will help Nepalis to help themselves.

Dress: A state of undress is unacceptable in both sexes. Men should not bare their chests in public, nor should women wear revealing blouses. Tight-fitting clothes should be avoided. Women should wear either a long loose skirt or slacks - not shorts.

Food: Do not touch food or utensils that Nepalis use. Never give or take food with the left hand, and should cutlery be unavailable, only use your right hand to eat with. When giving or receiving gifts it is considered polite to use both hands.

Haggling: In Kathmandu, haggling is part of the trade culture. On trek it is unacceptable to haggle over prices in tea-houses or lodges. Pay the going rate for food and lodging, which is usually set by the local community, but at the same time do not condone overcharging.

The hearth: Many hill-folk consider fires as sacred, so never discard rubbish onto your host's fire, no matter how small or insignificant it may seem. Nor should you sit next to the fire in a Nepali home unless invited to do so.

Legs & feet: The soles of your feet should not be pointed at a Nepali, nor should legs be so outstretched that they need to be stepped over. Feet are considered unclean.

Monasteries: When visiting monasteries remove boots or shoes before entering, and make a donation before leaving. In respect to local culture and belief, please refrain from smoking or noisy behaviour in or near a sacred site.

Photography: Be discreet when taking photographs of local people. Remember, you are not in a zoo, or a museum. Establish a relationship with your subject where possible, and ask permission before taking their photograph. Respect their right to say no. Do not promise to give

35

a copy of the photo you've taken unless you're certain you will be able to do so.

Prayer walls: Always pass to the left of a prayer wall (mani wall), chorten or stupa.

Short-cuts: Stick to trails and avoid trampling plants. Taking short-cuts can add to problems of soil erosion. Avoid walking in fields where crops are growing, and should you be faced with animals on the trail, make sure they pass on the downhill side.

Smile: A smile is international; act with patience and friendliness towards local people. Nepalis smile a lot, and that warmth should be reflected back.

Touching: Do not touch a Nepali on the head, and never touch anyone with your shoes. Pointing with your finger is considered to be rude; instead, use your right hand extended, with fingers together.

Wealth: Be discreet when handling money, and avoid tempting locals into envy by making an obvious display of the contents of your wallet. Keep a few small denomination rupee notes handy for paying bills along the way. Don't leave valuables unattended.

Finally, the word *Namaste*, given with palms pressed together in an attitude of prayer, is the universal greeting of Nepal. It means 'I salute the god within you' and will be well received when offered on the trail, in villages or in lodges and tea-houses. Use it with a smile - and mean it. You are offering a sign of respect. From such simple beginnings may grow a flower of understanding.

PRE-DEPARTURE PREPARATIONS

The traveller will save both time and money by planning his tour carefully before leaving home. (Karl Baedeker)

Seated outside a lodge in Chisopani eating lunch one day, I saw a young overweight trekker come staggering along the trail in a state of some distress. His face was streaked with sweat, his shirt soaked, his breath rasping as though he'd just completed a marathon. Dumping his rucksack on a wall he slumped in a heap in the shade, and when

at last he was able to speak began a long monologue of misery. His feet were badly blistered, his shoulders hurt, he was exhausted.

I eventually learnt that this was his first trek; his first-ever walking experience. He was a world-traveller adding Nepal to the list of countries to visit on his way to Thailand, and no-one had told him that trekking was like this. Someone had said Helambu was one of the easiest trekking regions; he had assumed it would entail wandering along level paths in the bed of a valley. But reality was different. It hurt and he was not enjoying it.

This book, along with others in the series of trekking guides to Nepal, has been produced, not to encourage more trekkers to explore the trails of the Langtang National Park, but hopefully to add something to the experience of those already committed to going there. Since it is better to be forewarned than to walk blindly into disappointment, this particular section should strip away the veneer of romance and expose the bare reality for those considering their first-ever trek in Nepal.

The overweight, blistered young man quoted above is not unique. The trails that lead among some of the highest mountains on earth attract a surprising number of people who have never undertaken a multi-day walk before, nor had even the bare minimum of mountain experience. That so many survive to return for more says as much about the spell cast by the fabled Himalaya as for the care and attention devoted to them by their trek organisers and crew.

Successful trekking may be described as the art of gaining most from the multitude of experiences on offer. But to achieve that requires as much mental preparation as physical fitness. Tackling a journey on foot that will demand two weeks or so of effort is a very different proposition to that of a fortnight's holiday based in one village from which to set out on day-walks as and when the mood arises. As a member of an organised group trek you will be expected to walk day after day, rain or shine, whether you feel up to it or not. So get yourself both mentally and physically fit before boarding the plane bound for Kathmandu.

Imagine, if you will, the following scenario: of waking one morning weary from past excesses and feeling queasy from a stomach upset. Imagine a cold wind blowing and a trek leader cajoling you to start walking. You have about eight hours of uphill trail ahead of you

37

before the next camp is set up - and there's no alternative but to pull on your boots and go.

There may well be occasions on trek in Langtang, Gosainkund or Helambu when you'll face a period of misery similar to that. Gosainkund can be bitterly cold, so can some of the high country leading to it from Helambu; and in Langtang too. There may be times when it's difficult to have a decent wash for several days at a stretch, or nights when you're unable to enjoy restful sleep. Perhaps you're slow to adapt to altitude; maybe the diet is not to your liking or, if you're new to camping, you discover that you dislike sleeping in a tent. (It happens, so do try a night or two camping out before you commit yourself to a trek that uses tents.) On a tea-house trek you could be dismayed by the standard of accommodation provided, or by the lack of hygiene. There will be times of confusion, of homesickness; times when your Western sensibilities are appalled by the different values accepted by those whose country you're wandering through.

Successful trekking demands an ability to adapt to a whole range of ever-changing circumstances, to put Western values on hold and be prepared to accept that there could be much to learn about living from Nepali hill culture. Learning to respect unfamiliar ways is in itself sometimes a shock to the system.

But if you're convinced that wandering among the most dramatic scenery on earth, of mingling daily with people of an entirely foreign culture, and that a sense of achievement at the end of the trek offer sufficient rewards for the odd day of misery or discomfort - then trekking is for you. If you have doubts - forget it. Five or six days into a long walk is not the time to decide that trekking was a mistake. The financial outlay required to undertake a trek in Nepal should be a sufficient spur to ensure that you enjoy every moment of your time there. Don't waste it on doubts or inadequate preparation.

As a member of an organised trek you have a duty to your fellow group members, and to the leader, to arrive in good shape and with fitness to match your enthusiasm. Trails are uncompromisingly steep in places, and there's only one real way to get physically fit for trekking in the Himalaya, and that is by walking up and down hills. Jogging will help build stamina and endurance, swimming and cycling are also beneficial. But walking uphill with a rucksack is the

best possible preparation. If hills are in short supply near your home, just walk as far and as often as you can wherever is convenient. Give up riding lifts and escalators, and walk up flights of stairs. Once you arrive in Nepal and the trail winds ahead as far as the eye can see, you'll be glad you put in some effort at home.

Having decided to go trekking, put most of your preconceived ideas behind you, open your eyes, your mind and your heart to all that Nepal has to offer, and set forth with a determination to see and to understand. You'll soon discover that the mountains are only part of the allure. As has been pointed out by a number of experienced trekkers in the past, few will be content with just one Himalayan journey. 'The trek of a lifetime' is likely to be the first of many.

EQUIPMENT CHECK-LIST

A change of flannel shirts and worsted stockings, a few pocket-handkerchiefs and the 'objets de toilette' may, with a little practice, be carried with hardly a perceptible increase of fatigue.
(Karl Baedeker)

Baedeker was writing in another age and with a rather different kind of traveller in mind, but some of his observations are as valid today for the modern trekker as they were for the visitor to the Alps in the late 19th century. He wrote, for example: "To be provided with enough and no more, may be considered the second golden rule of the traveller."

It is perhaps no bad thing that most airlines have a free baggage allowance of just 20kg (44lbs), for there is a tendency among some group trekkers to take far too much clothing and sundry equipment with them - knowing that with porters they'll not have to carry it themselves whilst on trek. Backpackers, on the other hand, will recognise the necessity of keeping the size and weight of their rucksacks to a minimum.

The following check-list will cover the requirements of most trekkers undertaking routes described in this book.

Rucksack (day-sack only for members of an organised group)

Kitbag (group trekkers only; these fit onto a porter's doko)

Boots (lightweight are best; also spare laces & cleaning kit)

Light shoes (trainers preferred)

Socks (outer & inner)

Trousers (light cotton for travel, hotel use & on trek; plus thicker pair for cold conditions

Long, loose skirt for women

Shirts (1 for travel, 2 or 3 for on trek)

Sweater (or fibre-pile jacket)

Down jacket (if going high, or late-season trekking)

Cagoule & overtrousers

Plastic bags

Penknife

Small padlock (to secure kitbag for group trekkers, or bedrooms if staying in lodges)

Water filter (optional for independents)

Underwear (include thermal wear for cold conditions)

Sleeping bag (4 seasons; also sleeping bag liner)

Insulation mat (Karrimat or similar)

Gloves

Woollen hat

Sunhat & sunglasses

Water bottle (1 litre capacity)

Headtorch (& spare bulb & batteries)

Mending kit

Toilet kit (include small towel)

Toilet paper (& lighter)

First Aid (see under Health Matters)

Map & compass

Guidebook

Notebook & pens

Whistle

Camera & films (plus spare batteries & lens tissues)

Passport (& passport photos)

Trekking pole / walking stick

Money belt

It's good to have a complete change of clothes waiting at the hotel in Kathmandu for your return from trek; most hotels have storage facilities, but make sure any baggage left behind is secure and clearly marked with your name and expected date of return.

A trekking pole has been included in the above list as experience proves their value in aiding balance on stream-crossings, on trails slippery with a morning glaze of ice, and on steep descents where they are particularly useful for anyone with problem knees. A trekking pole is really a ski stick in all but name. The best are lightweight but strong, and are telescopic so that the length can be quickly adjusted to suit. When reduced to minimum length they will often fit inside a kitbag or backpack for ease of transportation on airlines.

Nepal is an independent kingdom. Like Tibet it has always sought isolation and has secured it by excluding foreigners, of whom the most undesirable were white men. (H.W.Tilman)

Tilman was writing in 1949, since when much has changed in Nepal, especially with regard to the official attitude towards foreigners. However, bureaucracy in the East is like a dread disease and it's as well to be prepared for the various rules and regulations which, on their own, make trekking in the Himalaya a very different proposition to that of mountain holidays in Europe.

All foreigners, except Indian nationals, require a valid passport and tourist visa to enter Nepal. Visa applications should be made direct to the Nepalese Embassy or Consulate in your home country (see Appendix A). This is a straightforward process that involves minimal form-filling, the provision of two passport photographs and payment of the appropriate fee (check current prices with the Embassy). Postal applications should be made at least one month before the date of departure. Don't forget to include a stamped addressed envelope for the return of your passport. If you apply in person at the Embassy, be warned that you will not be able to collect your passport until the following day. Visas are valid for a period of three months after the date of issue, and have a duration of 30 days.

At present it is possible to obtain a 30-day visa upon arrival at Tribhuvan International Airport, Kathmandu. Unless there's a large queue, formalities are quickly dealt with. Application forms are available at the airport, but make sure you have passport photographs handy and the correct fee in US dollars.

Should you plan to spend more than 30 days in the country you'll need a visa extension. If you're part of an organised trek, your trekking company will arrange this on your behalf. But for independent travellers visa extensions must be purchased in Kathmandu at the Central Immigration Office on Tridevi Marg, between Kantipath and Thamel. Applications must be accompanied by passport, passport photographs and the appropriate fee. On occasion it may be necessary to show proof of the amount of foreign

currency exchanged within Nepal - sometimes the regulations insist you change a set sum for each day of your trek. This requirement changes from time to time with little advance warning, so be prepared by keeping bank exchange receipts, and make a photocopy of each one in case proof is demanded. Instant passport photo facilities, and photocopying machines, are situated near the Immigration Office in Kathmandu.

The amount of time foreigners are allowed to spend in Nepal during any given year fluctuates. Trek leaders and others who intend to spend several months there are advised to check with the Nepalese Embassy before finalising plans.

A trekking permit is required for all travel outside the Kathmandu Valley, Pokhara and Chitwan National Park. The fee for this is based upon the number of days for which it is valid - so much for each week on trek. The approved route is outlined on each permit by naming the main villages and districts to be visited. There are several checkpoints in the areas covered by this guide, and at each one permits must be submitted for inspection. Entry to the Langtang National Park also requires a permit. Both this and the trekking permit are issued at the Central Immigration Office.

Application forms are available at the office where a list of current rules and regulations is posted. Make sure you collect the correct form for Langtang, otherwise you can waste a lot of time queueing twice or more until you get it right! In addition to your passport and valid visa, you will need two passport photographs and, possibly, photocopies of bank exchange receipts - depending on regulations in force at the time. Applications can usually be dealt with the same day (check what time you must return to collect the permit), but at the height of the trekking season it may be necessary to wait several hours before permits are ready.

Offices are open Sunday to Thursday 10.00 to 14.00, and Friday morning from 10.00 till noon. Beware of the many official holidays and festivals that occur with some frequency and which can leave you kicking your heels for days whilst waiting for the office to re-open. In the main, autumn, trekking season queues are exceedingly long and progress seems painfully slow. However, the clerks dealing with an avalanche of applications work under considerable pressure and need your understanding, not expressions of frustration. (When

tempted to curse the bureaucratic form-filling and endless hours spent in queues, remember that it was during the days of the Raj that bureaucracy was introduced to the East - by Britain - and consider too the treatment handed out to certain foreign nationals by some immigration officials at major airports in Western capitals.)

If you cannot face the queues, or are short of time in Kathmandu to arrange everything, consider using an agent to obtain permits and visa extensions on your behalf. There are many agents with offices in Thamel and on Durbar Marg who will happily deal with the bureaucracy - for a fee. It will not be cheap, but you may well feel it is money worth spending. Do not be tempted to buy either trekking permits or visa extensions on the black market. Westerners have languished in Nepalese jails with plenty of time to regret having done so. The fee you pay for the privilege of trekking in Nepal is, after all, an important source of revenue for one of the poorest countries in the world.

HEALTH MATTERS

I felt dizzy and weak, and dangerous at both ends.
(Mike Harding)

The very activity of trekking should be beneficial to health, increasing your vitality and providing a wonderful sense of well-being. There are plenty of opportunities for restful sleep, while steady daily exercise in the grandest of all surroundings can be both physically and mentally stimulating, and lead to an enrichment of life. For a normal active person in good physical condition, trekking in Langtang, Gosainkund and Helambu should not present any undue health risk. Yet first-time visitors to the Himalaya often become obsessed by worries about their health, and there are occasions when the trails of Nepal seem like hypochondriacs' highways. Conversations in mess-tents, tea-houses and lodges alike zone in on topics related to bowel and bladder movement, on concerns related to the digestive tract, headaches, chest infections and the fear of altitude sickness. Obviously in a developing country the farther you wander from 'civilisation' the more important it is to look after your health, but don't allow these

concerns to become obsessive.

Prior to leaving home it would be wise for anyone with a particular reason for worry to undergo a thorough medical examination, and it is important to have those inoculations deemed necessary by the health authorities before you go. Take a first-aid kit with you, adopt a sensible attitude towards food and hygiene - and trust to luck. On the whole trekking is a healthy pursuit. Things will not be as they are at home, but if you expect there to be no risk at all when wandering in Nepal, save your money or book a holiday elsewhere.

Immunisation:

Unless you travel through an infected area on the way to Kathmandu, Nepal does not require visitors to show proof of immunisation. Vaccination against the following is, however, recommended: tuberculosis (BCG), typhoid, tetanus, meningitis and hepatitis. If your journey to Nepal passes through a region where yellow fever is prevalent, you must be vaccinated against this also. You may need to show a valid certificate of inoculation for this on entry. As certain vaccinations need to be taken some time before travelling, visit your doctor two or three months before your trek is due to commence.

Rabies exists in Nepal and there is a slight chance (estimated at 1 in 6000) that you might be bitten whilst in the country. Bearing in mind that the disease is fatal, you may wish to consider vaccination - it's rather expensive though. As a precaution do not approach or fuss dogs or monkeys.

Malaria:

If you plan to visit the Terai during your time in Nepal (perhaps Chitwan National Park is on your itinerary), or travel by way of Bangladesh or India, you may be advised to embark on a course of anti-malaria tablets. Check the requirement at least two weeks before going (see below). If advised, the normal dose is two tablets of Chloraquine per week, plus one daily tablet of Paludrine. (Check first with your doctor or pharmacist.) The course is usually started one week before arrival in an affected area, and continues for a month after leaving. Tablets are usually available over the counter from your local chemist.

Health Advice:

Up-to-date specialist advice can be obtained in the UK from MASTA (Medical Advisory Service for Travellers Abroad) who for a fee will send printed information in response to a telephone request. The number to call is: 0171 631 4408 (between 09.30 and 17.00 Monday to Friday). MASTA also operates a Travellers' Health Line which provides a health brief containing up-to-date information with regard to immunisations, malaria etc, and is tailored to specific journeys. (See Appendix A for address/telephone.)

Anyone with a record of lung or heart disease should avoid treks that go to high altitudes, and should consult their doctor before committing themselves to a trip to Nepal. It is in any case sensible to have a medical check before setting off on a lengthy Himalayan trek.

Chest Problems:

Coughs, colds and chest infections are exacerbated by smoky lodges, dust and the dry cold air of high altitude. The sound of locals emptying their lungs with a serenade of coughing and spitting is the hill music of Nepal, to which most trekkers add voice at some time or other. Soluble lozenges will soothe inflamed throats, catarrh pastilles are worth taking, as are antibiotics (Ampicillin, or as recommended) to combat chest infections.

Water:

The most frequent cause of health problems is contaminated water. With poor sanitation a variety of organisms live in the streams and rivers of Nepal, and *all water should be considered suspect* (including that supplied in hotels and restaurants in Kathmandu) unless it has been vigorously boiled for ten minutes, treated with iodine or comes in a bottle with an unbroken seal. Certain advanced water filtration systems, such as the portable Katadyn filter, claim to be effective even in eliminating giardia cysts, and could be worth using in the hills.

Iodine (Lugol's solution - available in Kathmandu pharmacies) is most often used by trekkers to treat suspect water, and should be carried in a small dropper bottle protected against spillage in several polythene bags. Five to eight drops per litre is the recommended amount. Leave for 20-30 minutes (longer for very cold or cloudy

water) before drinking. Many iodine bottles sold in Kathmandu have faulty screw tops, and you are advised to transfer the contents to a more leak-proof container.

On a group trek in the care of a reputable adventure travel company, the leader should see that the cook and kitchen crew make every effort to ensure that all water is properly treated, and you should have no concerns on this score. However, if you are relying on food and drink from tea-houses and lodges, it is advisable be more circumspect. Beware milk drinks and the local brew (*chang* or *tomba*), and consume only those liquids you can be sure have been adequately boiled. Tea, for example, is usually safe.

Remember too to use only sterilized water when cleaning your teeth.

Giardia:

Giardia lamblia is a tiny protozoan parasite prevalent in the streams of upland Nepal - and in many other parts of the world too (ie, it is not limited to developing countries). When digested the parasite invades the upper part of the small intestine; it can damage the gut lining, and is fairly common among trekkers. After infection it may take two or three weeks before symptoms become apparent, and may result in sudden acute illness, or have a more long-lasting effect. One sure way of identifying a giardia sufferer is by the foul-smelling, rotten-egg gases emitted. Although not life-threatening, giardia is still a major health risk - and it strains friendships. Symptoms include nausea, feeling bloated, stomach cramps after eating, weight loss and dehydration. Irregular bouts of diarrhoea accompanied by pale, greasy mucus also form part of the symptom, but treatment is straightforward and fairly rapid. A course of tinidazole antibiotic (Tiniba is the brand name available in Kathmandu pharmacies) normally results in a complete cure: 2gr in a single dose daily for three days. This should be taken one hour before food.

Food and Hygiene:

Food is another potential problem area for independent trekkers, but with a little luck and forethought you should remain mostly trouble-free. Try to avoid uncooked fruit unless you can peel it yourself, salad vegetables that may have been rinsed in untreated water, and any

foods that may have been cooked earlier and later reheated.

Most trekkers suffer a mild dose of diarrhoea (Kathmandu Quickstep) at some time or other during their stay in Nepal, although this is often simply reaction to a change of diet. Sufferers need not become unduly alarmed unless blood is passed in the stools (a sign of possible dysentery), for this usually remedies itself in a few days. Take plenty of liquids to prevent dehydration, reduce solid food intake and avoid dairy products and alcohol. A rehydration solution, such as Dioralyte or Jeevan Jal (the Nepalese brand on sale in Kathmandu) is quickly absorbed into the system and will help speed recovery.

Basic rules of hygiene, such as washing hands thoroughly before meals and after going to the toilet, are obvious but should not be overlooked.

All food and drinks consumed in Kathmandu should be treated with the same circumspection as on trek. Many trekkers are fine throughout their time in the mountains, but relax their guard on return to city restaurants where they indulge in a spree of joyful gluttony. Then suffer for it. The time to relax your guard is when you arrive home. That being said, do keep your concerns in perspective and don't allow them to dominate your time in Nepal. With a little forethought and detail to personal hygiene, you should remain perfectly fit and healthy.

Mountain Sickness:

The other major concern of trekkers is that of altitude, or mountain, sickness. Acute Mountain Sickness (AMS) can affect anyone above an altitude of about 2000 metres (6500ft), but it is not possible to predict in advance who will suffer from it. Physical fitness, apparently, has little bearing upon it; nor has age. In fact it would appear that young people may be more susceptible to AMS than older trekkers, although this may be due to the eagerness of some young and fit walkers to gain height too rapidly.

AMS occurs as a result of the body failing to acclimatise adequately to reduced oxygen levels experienced at altitude. Apart from such high crossings as the Ganja La and Tilman's Pass, treks described in this book remain at fairly modest altitudes, but attention to the possibility of AMS should always be there. Nowhere along the trails

of Langtang, Gosainkund or Helambu is too high for a normal healthy individual to acclimatise without undue difficulty, although some take much longer than others to adapt. By failing to allow sufficient time for acclimatisation, AMS is almost guaranteed to develop. The best way to avoid it is to ascend gradually once you reach 2000 metres (6500ft), and above 3000 metres (10,000ft) ascend no more than about 400 metres (1300ft) per day. Depending on your chosen route and ambitions for exploration at altitude, it may not be easy to follow the golden rule of 'climb high, sleep low' so it is important to make height gain gradually, with occasional rest days, in order to allow the body to acclimatise properly.

At altitude it is important to avoid dehydration. The recommended liquid intake is at least 4 litres (7 pints) a day, and to urinate a minimum of half a litre per day - a great deal of fluid is lost at altitude through breathing. Yellow-coloured urine is a sign that liquid intake needs to be increased.

With the onset of AMS fluid accumulates in the lungs or the brain or, in extreme cases, in both. Recognising the symptoms, and attention to reducing them, are both vital if serious illness or, at worst, death is to be avoided. Early signs of AMS to watch for are extreme fatigue, headache and loss of appetite. Some trekkers also find they become breathless with only minimal exercise, and suffer disturbed sleep. When these symptoms develop do not go any higher until they have gone away. If they show no sign of leaving after a day or two, but instead become worse, it is important to descend to lower levels. Do not take sleeping tablets or strong pain killers, since these can mask some of the symptoms.

A worsening condition is indicated by vomiting, severe headache, lack of co-ordination, wet, bubbly breathing, increased tiredness and breathlessness even at rest. Such symptoms warn of the onset of a very serious condition which, if ignored, can lead to loss of consciousness and death within 12 hours. The only known cure, if acted upon in time, is to *descend at once* until symptoms decrease and finally disappear completely. An improvement will normally be felt after 300 metres (1000ft) or so of descent.

High Altitude Cerebral Edema (HACE) and High Altitude Pulmonary Edema (HAPE) occur as advanced stages of AMS and are both potential killers. Every year a number of trekkers die in Nepal

through failure to recognise and respond to the symptoms. The only cure is either immediate descent to lower altitudes or, if one is available, to insert the patient into a Gamow Bag in which pressure is raised by means of a foot pump to simulate a lower altitude. In the case of HACE or HAPE no patient should be left to descend alone; nor should there be any delay. If symptoms occur at night do not even wait until morning to descend.

As with all health concerns it is important to be aware of potential dangers, but keep them in perspective and do not allow your concerns to devalue the pleasures of the trek. Be aware of symptoms, act upon them if and when they occur and, time and energy willing, continue with your trek when signs of improvement indicate it is safe to do so.

Detailed advice may be gleaned from reading James A. Wilkerson's *Medicine for Mountaineering* (The Mountaineers) or Peter Steele's *Medical Handbook for Mountaineers* (Constable).

Hospitals, Health Posts and Emergency Evacuation:

The Himalayan Rescue Association (HRA) has an office in Kathmandu (situated near the Central Immigration Office on Tridevi Marg) which is worth a visit before going on trek. Not only will you receive good advice with regard to AMS and other health matters, but forms are available to enable you to register with your Embassy, which can be useful in an emergency.

There are no health posts in the regions covered by this guide, and the nearest hospital out of the Kathmandu Valley is situated in Trisuli Bazaar. For emergency evacuation there is a STOL (Short Take-Off and Landing) airstrip in the Langtang Valley just beyond Kyangjin Gompa, but flights are dependent on good weather conditions and should not be relied upon. Evacuation by air *in an emergency* may be possible, but could be difficult to organise and will be extremely expensive to carry out. Rescues will only be attempted when a guarantee of payment has been made. It has been said that if you're trekking in a group with a reputable company and something goes wrong it may be possible to arrange emergency evacuation by helicopter. If you're travelling independently, there's little or no chance.

There are radio stations at Ghora Tabela, Rasuwa Garhi on the Bhote Kosi by the Tibetan border, and at Dhunche.

Should you need to consult a Western doctor on your return to Kathmandu, the best-known place for consultations is the Canadian-run CIWEC clinic opposite the Russian Embassy in Baluwatar (tel: 410983). Consulting hours are: Monday to Friday 09.00-12.00 and 13.00-15.30; expensive, but facilities are said to be good.

First-Aid Kit:

All trekkers, whether travelling independently or with an organised group, should carry a personal first-aid kit, the very minimum contents of which should be:

Elastoplast or similar dressing strips

Butterfly closures

Bandages (cotton gauze & elastic)

Throat lozenges & cough pastilles

Iodine (in plastic dropper bottle)

Immodium (or similar for diarrhoea relief)

Antibiotic (Ciproxin, Ampicillin or as prescribed)

Rehydration solution (Dioralyte or Jeevan Jal)

Emergency dental kit

Moleskin (for blisters)

Antiseptic cream

Paracetamol (or Aspirin)

Low reading thermometer

Sun cream

Lip salve

Tiniba (to combat giardia)

Scissors

Safety pins

Also recommended is a pack of sterile needles for use in emergencies where injections may be necessary. This will help reduce the risk of accidental transmission of HIV (AIDS) and Hepatitis B viruses through contaminated equipment. MASTA (see above) produces a sterile medical equipment pack that contains syringes, sutures and dressings as well as needles.

A copy of *The Himalayan First Aid Manual* by Jim Duff and Peter Gormly, available from KEEP in Kathmandu, is also worth carrying. This slim, pocket-sized manual is packed with useful information.

Most medicines, including antibiotics, are readily available without prescription in Kathmandu - a number of general pharmacies are located on New Road and in various parts of Thamel. Do not rely on the diagnostic advice of untrained pharmacists (some are well-qualified, though); where doubts occur seek medical assistance.

Make sure you have all you might expect to need in the way of medical aid before setting out on trek.

MAPS

Maps, even those with contour lines, fail to give the correct impression of slopes on mountain terrain. (Harka Gurung)

The Langtang, Gosainkund and Helambu regions are covered by a variety of maps available in Kathmandu, some of which are also obtainable in the UK (see the Appendix for addresses of map suppliers). Most of these, it must be said, leave a lot to be desired with regard to accuracy. The shortcomings on some sheets include outdated trail routes, misplaced villages and the confusing way of indicating solitary tea-houses in type normally associated with important villages. Altitudes often vary from sheet to sheet, and spellings vary too. However, for general trekking purposes, for general day-to-day travel on the clear, well-trodden trails, they should be adequate. If the maps do not match the standards of cartography you've become used to at home, see that as an advantage; confusion only adds to the adventure. As has been noted earlier, in Nepal the important thing to remember when orienting yourself is the name of the next village or pass. If you are unsure of which way to go, simply ask directions from the first person you meet. (When doing this, be careful not to ask: "Is this the way to...?" But rather, "Which is the trail to...?")

The fanciest maps of Langtang are the two sheets of Alpenvereinskarte published under the title *Langthang Himal* at a scale of 1:50,000. The western sheet covers the area from Dhunche to Kyangjin; includes Gosainkund lakes to Laurebina La at the southern extreme, and overlaps into Tibet in the north. The eastern sheet (Öst) covers the upper Langtang Valley east of Kyangjin, with the Ganja La also shown. This sheet also overlaps into Tibet in the north.

The so-called 'Schneider' map, published in Vienna by Freytag-Berndt/Artaria, and named after the man who undertook the first survey here, is titled *Helambu-Langtang* at a scale of 1:100,000.

Mandala Productions in Kathmandu produce a single dyeline sheet in their series 'Latest Trekking Map' which covers all the area

described in this book. *Helambu, Gosainkund, Langtang, Ganja La* is published at a scale of 1:125,000, with contours at 250 metre intervals. Note that even the most recent edition depicts one or two trails that have fallen into misuse, while at least one major present-day path does not appear at all.

Mandala Maps (not to be confused with the above-named) have a four-colour sheet at 1:100,000 entitled *Helambu-Langtang, Gosainkund* and covering a similar area to the previously mentioned map. Trail depiction is also suspect and some altitudes quoted are very questionable. However, as with other sheets mentioned, it has a modest value in providing a rough overview of these particular trekking regions.

Italian cartographer Paolo Gondini has created a series of trekking maps for Nepa Publications (available in Kathmandu) under the sub-heading 'For Extreme and Soft Trekking'. The *Langtang* sheet at 1:120,000 covers Langtang, Helambu and Gosainkund, and differs from others mentioned above by the inclusion of symbols depicting various features: waterfalls, hot springs, gompas, caves, etc. Also included is a very simple route profile.

Finally, the lodge owner of Hotel Langtang View in Dhunche has produced a useful double-sided sheet which is basically a simple sketch map showing the route through the Langtang Valley, and on the reverse side trekking routes through Helambu, on which the various lodges and villages have been marked, with a note of estimated times between each establishment added. Route profiles are also given. Available from Hotel Langtang View, Dhunche.

GETTING THERE

"Kathmandu flight going yesterday - next time going in four days." (quoted by Bill O'Connor)

By Air:

Currently Nepal is served by eight international airlines. Among those flying from Europe are: Royal Nepal Airlines Corporation (RNAC), Biman Bangladesh , Pakistan International Airlines (PIA), Lufthansa and Aeroflot.

RNAC operate twice-weekly flights from London, calling at Frankfurt and Dubai. In advance of the main trekking seasons they become heavily booked, so plan well ahead if you hope to travel with them. Royal Nepal also arrange charter flights.

Flights by Biman and PIA involve connections in Dhaka and Karachi respectively. Biman at present offer among the cheapest tickets but be warned that on occasion an unannounced delay of 24 hours or more can leave passengers frustrated in Dhaka. Lufthansa fly Frankfurt to Kathmandu via Dubai, while Aeroflot fly London to Kathmandu via Moscow; no frills and cheapest prices.

Other flights can be arranged that require connections via India. Unfortunately the bureaucracy involved in transit at Delhi Airport can be extremely tedious.

Return flights out of Kathmandu are nearly always fully booked during the main trekking seasons. It is essential to reconfirm homeward flights at least 72 hours before departure time. Failure to do so may lead to the loss of your seat, even though you have a ticket, and you will then have plenty of time to regret the omission. The safest course is to reconfirm as soon as you arrive in Kathmandu, and again upon return from trek. Before spending the last of your Nepalese currency, check the amount of departure tax to be paid at the airport. The precise amount depends on your destination.

By Other Means:

Travellers heading for Nepal from India will find that a combination of rail and road travel can take as much as three days for the journey from Delhi to Kathmandu via Agra, Varanasi, Patna and the border crossing at Birganj. Coming from Darjeeling it is possible to take an Indian train to Siliguri, and taxi from there to the border post at Kakar Bhitta in the eastern Terai. Buses ply the route from Kakar Bhitta to Kathmandu along the Mahendra Highway.

Entry by road from Tibet is by way of Kodari (Khasa on the Tibetan side), but this crossing is often closed by landslide during the monsoon, and made difficult by officialdom at other times. Before going to Tibet in the first place, check the current situation with regard to a return journey to Nepal.

Note that all vehicles entering Nepal must have an international *carnet de passage*.

Travel Within Nepal:

Bicycle rickshaws offer the cheapest form of transport in Kathmandu. They provide a bumpy, uncomfortable ride for one or two people but are worth considering if you've lost your way in town and need to get back to your hotel.

Next in line are the fume-belching three-wheeled Tempos. With seating for two and a meter that seldom works, they are only marginally cheaper to hire than taxis, and have difficulty getting uphill. If you want to ride to Swayambunath, for example, and you don't fancy pushing, you'd better think in terms of a taxi.

By Western standards taxis are also cheap to use in and around town and throughout the Kathmandu Valley, and are ideal for sightseeing purposes. It can often be worth hiring a taxi for a whole day (agree a price first), especially if you plan to visit a number of sites.

Public buses provide an 'interesting' and extremely cheap mode of transport. Unbelievably crowded, discomfort is guaranteed as the seats are designed with the Nepalese in mind, who as a race are generally several inches shorter than Europeans. Occasionally seats have a bit of padding, but often they don't. On a long journey it is virtually certain that several of your fellow passengers will be overcome by travel sickness and watch the miles slowly pass by as they throw up out of the windows. Although against the law to do so, it is often more pleasant to spend the journey on the roof-top along with piles of baggage.

Public buses service the route from Kathmandu to Dhunche (for Langtang and Gosainkund) via Trisuli Bazaar, as well as the shorter journey to Sundarijal (for Helambu). Tourist buses also go to Dhunche and at least provide a little more leg room. Since the road from Trisuli Bazaar is unpaved (the road from Kathmandu to Trisuli is not much better since it's breaking up through lack of maintenance), the 112 kilometre (70 mile) journey will take all day, including a *daal bhat* stop along the way. Inevitable delays are also created by an assortment of checkpoints where foreigners need to show their trekking permits and enter details in a ledger.

NEPAL - FACTS AND FIGURES

None of the books or photographs studied before leaving home had even slightly prepared me for such majesty. (Dervla Murphy)

Rectangular in shape and measuring roughly 800 by 240 kilometres (500 x 150 miles), Nepal contains the largest number of 8000 metre peaks (26,000ft) in the world. But mountains form only the northern part of this beautiful country, for in the south lies the tropical belt of the Terai - an extension of the Gangetic plain - while the broad central region is one of fertile hills rising from 600 to 2000 metres (2000-6500ft) in altitude. The sub-tropical Kathmandu Valley is included in this central strip, as are neighbouring valley basins.

Nepal is the world's only Hindu monarchy. Official statistics suggest that of a population of around 19 million, some 90% are Hindu, and just 8% of the Buddhist faith. Yet **Hindu and Buddhist** co-exist in harmony here, and merge compatibly in so many different ways that it is not always easy to separate them. When trekking in the mountains, especially in Langtang, one sees constant evidence of Buddhism, with chortens, prayer flags, gompas and mani walls providing a constant reminder of a tradition of spirituality contained within this once-remote haven of peace and beauty.

The official **language**, Nepali, is derived from Pahori which comes from northern India and is spoken by some 58% of the population. But it has been pointed out that there are as many different languages in Nepal as there are races, and as many dialects as there are villages. In the Kathmandu Valley the original language of Newari uses no less than three different alphabets. Fortunately for the Western trekker English is widely understood not only in Kathmandu but in many lodges along the popular trails and among senior members of a Nepalese trek crew. A brief glossary of Nepali words will be found in the Appendix.

Although Nepal numbers among the poorest nations on earth in terms of per capita income, the trekker here does not experience the same sense of hopeless poverty that is so prevalent in a number of other Eastern countries. The majority of the population (over 80%) depend for their livelihood on **agriculture**, much of which is

subsistence farming on the intricate terraced fields of the hill country. Some 17% of land is under cultivation, and about 30% covered in forest. However, the demands of a fast-growing population (a 2.1% rise annually) and a corresponding increase in livestock have changed Nepal from being a net exporter of food to a net importer. Year by year the food deficit is widening, productivity is actually declining, and there's been a marked reduction in forests that needs to be arrested. Nepal now faces serious economic and environmental problems which only considered development can address.

Whilst foreign development projects pour money into Nepal, some of these schemes are of questionable value. Charlie Pye-Smith's book *Travels in Nepal* provides an interesting commentary on the question of **foreign aid** here, and *The Rough Guide to Nepal* also includes one or two sobering articles that are worth reading by anyone interested in the question of development aid.

Tourism is the largest source of earned income, although only 2% of the population find active employment within it. Trekking, of course, forms an important part of the tourist industry and provides much-needed foreign currency, but a considerable slice of the money you pay for a group trek organised by a Western agency never reaches Nepal.

International **telecommunication** is made possible through the British earth satellite station installed in 1982. Telephone connections with Europe and the United States are good, and are widely available in Kathmandu where a number of small offices offering telephone, telex and fax facilities are to be found in Thamel and other tourist haunts (look for signs emblazoned with the initials: ISD/STD/IDD). Most hotels and trekking agencies in the capital are now accessible by fax.

Nepalese **time** is 5 hours 45 minutes ahead of Greenwich Mean Time (15 minutes ahead of Indian Standard Time), 12 hours 45 minutes ahead of New York, 15 hours 45 minutes ahead of Los Angeles, and 21 hours 45 minutes ahead of Sydney, Australia.

Postal services are dealt with in Kathmandu at the General Post Office located at the junction of Kantipath and Kicha-Pokhari Road. The office is open daily (except Saturdays and public holidays) from 10.00 to 17.00 (16.00 November to February). When posting always ensure that stamps on postcards, letters and parcels are franked by

the counter clerk. There is invariably a queue at the special counter reserved for franking stamps. Some reliable Kathmandu hotels and guest houses will take mail to the post office for you. Never mail anything in a public postbox. Expect letters and cards to take anything upwards of ten days to be delivered.

Poste Restante facilities are available at the GPO in Kathmandu, and are quite efficient. Send post with the name of the recipient clearly marked, and with the surname either underlined or printed in capital letters, c/o Poste Restante, GPO, Kathmandu, Nepal. The Poste Restante facility is a self-service affair. In a room set aside for this, mail is filed alphabetically in large trays where you can help yourself. Mail is held here for around two months.

The local **currency** is the Rupee (Rps) which consists of 100 Paisa. As a 'soft' currency it has no exchange value outside Nepal, and should not be taken out of the country. Travellers' cheques and 'hard' currency can be exchanged at Tribhuvan International Airport on arrival, and at a number of banks which are open daily except Saturdays, from 10.00 until about 14.00. Always collect your exchange receipts as these may be needed when applying for trekking permits or visa extensions. Make a point of accumulating plenty of small-denomination notes for use on trek; it is no good stopping at a trailside tea-house a week's walk from the nearest bank and expect to pay for your cup of tea with a Rps500 or Rps1000 note.

TIME IN KATHMANDU

And the wildest dreams of Kew are the facts of Kathmandu.
(Rudyard Kipling)

Despite all the obvious problems and disadvantages of an Eastern capital growing too fast for its own good, Kathmandu remains one of the world's most magical cities and it is worth devoting a few days, either before or after trek, to absorbing its unique atmosphere and explore neighbouring towns within the valley. After weeks spent among the mountains it is a great place to sample a change of menu too, for there are dozens of restaurants to satisfy all appetites. There are numerous hotels and guest-houses of varying degrees of comfort,

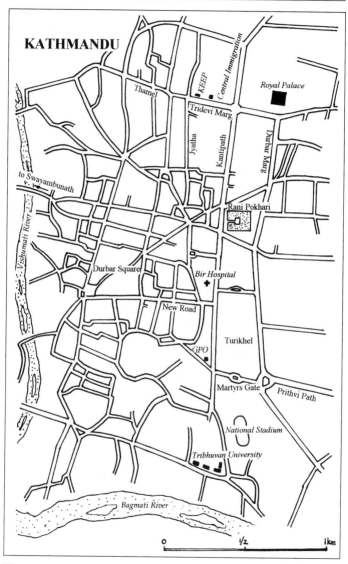

KATHMANDU

Thamel

KEEP

Central Immigration

Royal Palace

Tridevi Marg

Jyatha

Kantipath

Durbar Marg

to Swayambunath

Vishnumati River

Rani Pokhari

Durbar Square

Bir Hospital

New Road

GPO

Turikhel

Martyrs Gate

Prithvi Path

National Stadium

Tribhuvan University

Bagmati River

0   ½   1 km

and enough shops and street traders offering a thousand and one 'bargains' to help you spend the last of your money.

Kathmandu's hotels range from the fancy and comparatively high-priced, such as those on Durbar Marg - Hotel Sherpa with its floor shows, Hotel de l'Annapurna with its sauna and swimming pool, and the Yak and Yeti with its opulent restaurants - to an array of unpretentious lodgings stuffed away in Thamel back streets or on the one-time hippy hideout of Freak Street. Popular middle-range accommodation includes the perennial favourite of the Kathmandu Guest House in the heart of Thamel, and the Mustang Holiday Inn hidden round the back of Jyatha. Jyatha is lined with numerous medium- and low-priced hotels sought out mostly by independent travellers, while the Yellow Pagoda beside busy Kantipath is heavily used by trekking groups from the UK. There should be no difficulty in finding accommodation at a price to suit. Just head for Thamel or Jyatha and pick one that attracts. If a first night doesn't agree with you, move on until you find a place that does.

For a thousand years and more Kathmandu profited from its control of the main trade route between India and Tibet. Rimmed with hills and encircled by rivers the city, badly damaged by earthquake on 15 January 1934, draws ever-larger numbers of the population from the outlying hills, for in Nepal, as in countries throughout the world, there are those who imagine the streets of the capital city to be paved with gold. But Kathmandu suffers from traffic pollution, an inadequate water supply, unreliable electricity supply and no proper underground sewage system. In the 1870s David Wright, a surgeon at the British Residency, produced a report which cynics might consider apt today. It read: "The streets of Kathmandu are very narrow, mere lanes in fact; and the whole town is very dirty...to clean the drains would be impossible without knocking down the entire city...In short, from a sanitary point of view, Kathmandu may be said to be built on a dunghill in the middle of latrines."

That is but one view. Kathmandu is a cornucopia of colour, of smells, of noise. It *is* dirty. But it's also exciting, vibrant, lively. A dull cloud of pollution hangs over the city, yet below it there's often unrestrained gaiety. In countless streets medieval buildings are adorned with carvings of delicate and timeless beauty. There are

people everywhere, the narrow alleyways and broad modern streets acrush with activity. Traffic streams in an endless honking procession through the daylight hours along the main highways. Bicycle rickshaws, motor-bikes, tempos and taxis bounce and weave through the teeming streets of Thamel, and manage somehow to avoid collision with crowds of traders, bustle of porters, tourists and beggars - and the occasional cow.

Thamel is the ever-popular tourist district in the north-west of the city, a brazen mis-match of building styles, curiously-worded hoardings, hash-touting wide boys, carpet salesmen, flute sellers and bleary-eyed world travellers. In addition to its plentiful supply of budget accommodation, there's a fine selection of restaurants and bookshops, suppliers of climbing and trekking equipment, outfitters of all kinds, and a specialist trekker's food shop. If your airline has sent your baggage to Karachi by mistake, you'll find all you need in the shop-lined streets of Thamel.

But it is the wealth of religious and cultural sites that puts Kathmandu in a category all its own and makes the town so appealing. "There are nearly as many temples as houses, and as many idols as inhabitants," wrote William Kirkpatrick in 1811, and while there are certainly more houses and inhabitants today - plus a great many tourists - there is no shortage of places to visit, either in the capital itself, or in the neighbouring towns of Patan and Bhaktapur and throughout the Kathmandu Valley. The following suggestions merely scratch the surface. For more detailed information, background history and as a pointer to the full glories of the valley, the *Insight Guide to Nepal* (APA Publications) is highly recommended.

Kathmandu:

Durbar Square is a must, and is the obvious place from which to begin an exploration of the city for it contains more than fifty important monuments, shrines and temples, as well as the huge Hanuman Dhoka (Royal Palace), providing a superb roofscape of exotic shapes. Intricate carvings adorn every building: erotic figures, faces, patterns and religious symbols have been delicately etched on practically every strut and beam and around each doorway and window, by generations of Newari craftsmen. Early morning is the best time to visit. Street vendors are setting out their wares, porters

gather to await employment, the faithful scurry to various temples for their first devotions of the day, and the place comes alive with streams of light, colour and movement. By mid-morning the Square is crowded.

Make a point of visiting the **Hanuman Dhoka.** One of the pagoda-like turrets (Besantapur Tower) serves as a lookout and provides an amazing view of the town spread out below, and of the distant Langtang Himal to the north. At the south-western corner of the Square, the **Kasthamandap** is reckoned to be one of the oldest wooden buildings in the world. Tradition has it that it was constructed in the 12th century from a single tree, and for centuries served as a rest house for travellers plying the trade route to Tibet. The inner courtyard of nearby **Kumari Chowk,** home of the 'living goddess' the Raj Kumari, is richly carved with exquisite pillars, doors and windows, while the lofty 16th century **Taleju Mandir** temple, rising above the eastern side of the Square from a twelve-tiered plinth, was designed as Kathmandu's highest building.

To the north of Durbar Square, midway between the Square and Thamel, and secluded off the busy street of Shukrapath, stands the biggest stupa of central Kathmandu. **Kathesimbhu** is a colourful gathering place for Buddhist monks, tourists and the children of a neighbouring school who use the surrounding space as a playground. There's another stupa, a low modest one, standing in a square to the north of this, with street traders squatting among their wares at its base.

On a site considered sacred more than 2500 years ago, the Buddha's eyes painted on the great stupa of **Swayambhunath** (Swayambhu) look down on Kathmandu from a hilltop perch west of the Vishumati river. A long flight of some 300 stone steps leads to the stupa among trees where monkeys play, and from the top a grand view overlooks the valley. A row of prayer wheels encircles the stupa, and behind it a gompa, or monastery, attracts visitors. Inside, hundreds of butter lamps flicker while drums, gongs and trumpets accompany each devotion. The stupa is surrounded by an assortment of bells, shrines, statues and other symbolic objects; there's a small gilt temple dedicated to the smallpox goddess, Harati, a museum and a Buddhist library.

The Vishumati river flows round the western side of Kathmandu,

The eyes of the Buddha look out over Kathmandu

while the Bagmati twists along the eastern boundary and is straddled by **Pashupatinath**, the most important Hindu pilgrim site in all Nepal. As a tributary of the Ganges the Bagmati is considered sacred by devout Hindus, and ritual bathing here is thought to be especially meritorious. Above the river a temple complex remains out of bounds to non-Hindus, but on the east bank a series of terraces provides viewpoints from which to study not only the gilded temple, but also the riverside activities below. In the river itself women do their laundry, while Hindus fast approaching death are carried from the nearby *dharmsalas* (rest houses) and lain on stone slabs with their feet in the water until all life has drained from them. Nearby ghats are used by commoners for cremation, others are reserved for the use of royalty. Cremations are conducted by the families of the deceased, and although these are carried out in full public view, tourists should act with sensitivity and avoid intruding with cameras and prying eyes. Near-naked Sadhus drift among the buildings, while the whole complex swarms with pilgrims during the new moon festival of Shiva Raatri held in late February/early March.

North-east of Kathmandu, and a little north of Pashupatinath, the great Buddhist stupa of **Bodhnath** (Boudha or Boudhanath) is one of

the world's largest, its huge dome measuring 40 metres in height (130ft) seen from afar and marking the centre of Tibetan culture in Nepal. Monasteries and pilgrim rest houses cluster around, and at the start of the Tibetan New Year (February) monks take part in colourful ceremonies here. Masked dances are performed for the public in a nearby field, while other dances take place in a monastery courtyard.

Patan:

South of Kathmandu, and divided from it only by the Bagmati river, the once-independent kingdom of Patan (Lalitpur) is a very old town founded, it is claimed, in the third century BC by the emperor Ashoka and his daughter Carumati. Primarily a Buddhist town it boasts around 150 former monasteries, but there are also many Hindu temples and shrines and scores of exotic secular buildings, so that it would take weeks of concentrated study to properly visit each one.

This 'town of a thousand golden roofs' has its own **Durbar Square** with the former Royal Palace facing a complex variety of Newari architectural wonders. The Palace itself has three main courtyards open to the public, each one displaying the skills of woodcarvers of past generations. Nearby the beautiful Buddhist monastery, **Kwa Bahal** (otherwise known as the Hiranyavarna Mahavihara, or Golden Temple), dates from the 12th century and, with its ornate statues and gilded roofs, is worth seeking out - but remember to remove your footwear before stepping into the lower courtyard.

Jawalakhel, on the south-western edge of Patan, is where many Tibetans have settled following the Chinese invasion of their country in the 1950s. A thriving carpet factory has been established here which is usually on the itinerary of busloads of tourists.

Like Kathmandu, Patan is a bustling town with a vibrancy all its own. A town of artisans, metalwork is a speciality, the narrow alleys and side streets ringing to the sound of hammer or file on copper and tin. Once you've absorbed as much spiritual and architectural wonder as you can, stroll around the tiny workshops where local craftsmen pick out ornamental filigree with hammer and punch, or spend an hour or so in the bazaars and enjoy haggling for bargains with the street vendors.

Bhaktapur:

Also known by its former name of Bhadgaon, this handsome town of about 50,000 residents lies 16 kilometres (10 miles) to the east of Kathmandu. Described by Percival Landon as "willingly remote from her neighbours, and one of the most picturesque towns in the East", it's reached by a pleasant journey from the capital through open country, then climbing among pine trees and alongside two small reservoirs on the outskirts of the town itself. If you arrive by bus, however, you'll be dropped about ten minutes' walk to the south of town.

Badly damaged in 1934 by the same earthquake that devastated Kathmandu, Bhaktapur nevertheless retains much of its medieval character and is unquestionably the finest town in the valley with regard to architectural delights. Much of the restoration work has been made possible through a German-Nepalese development project that has so far helped preserve some 200 buildings without destroying their essential character. Some of the best will be seen in and around **Durbar Square** which is entered through a gateway on its western edge. This provides a broad open approach to a magnificent collection of temples and monuments, with the **Golden Gate** (Sun Dhoka) catching the eye as a vibrant masterpiece leading into the Taleju Chowk. At least two large temples in the Square were completely destroyed by the earthquake, but those that remain are set out with sufficient space to enable the visitor to study them from different angles without their being confused among other crowded buildings.

Whilst Durbar Square is considered by many to be the main focus of attention in Bhaktapur, a short stroll of about 100 metres to the south-east leads to **Taumadhi Tol**, surrounded by lovely old Newari houses and dominated by the pagoda-like **Nyatapola Temple**, Bhaktapur's tallest, which stands on a five-stepped pedestal guarded by a succession of stone wrestlers, elephants, lions, griffins and goddesses. A fine view of this, and the rest of the square, is obtained from one of the balconies of the Cafe Nyatapola, in itself a delightful building.

The oldest part of the town lies east of Durbar Square. Here **Tachapol Tol** (Tacapal or Dattatraya Square) has two old, but not

Langtang Lirung (7245m: 23,770ft) seen from the summit of Kyangjin Ri

The southern wall of the Langtang Valley beyond Kyangjin
The upper Langtang Valley near Nubamatang

particularly elaborate temples, Dattatraya and Bhimsen, and a slender pillar-statue of Garud. Linked to the rest of town by narrow alleyways, there is much to explore in Tachapol Tol. Take special note of the magnificent carvings that adorn so many buildings, particularly around the windows and doorways of the 18th century **Pujari Math** where the lattice-work of the famed **Peacock Window** is perhaps the most celebrated piece of woodwork in the Kathmandu Valley. The art of the woodcarver here has reached the very height of perfection.

Finally, if you have a few days to spare after trek, consider heading out to either **Dhulikhel** or **Nagarkot** for a more peaceful wind-down than may be won from Kathmandu, and more importantly to gain mid-distant views of the Himalayan chain running along the horizon.

Dhulikhel nestles in a saddle of hills about 30 kilometres (19 miles) east of Kathmandu at an altitude of about 1550 metres (5085ft). There are several hotels catering for tourists who visit in order to enjoy the glories of sunrise over the Himalaya. For the best views you'll need to walk for about 45 minutes or so south-east of Dhulikhel to gain the summit of a 1715 metre (5627ft) hill. From there a remarkable panorama stretches from Annapurna to Everest, with Langtang and Helambu forming the central portion of the view.

Nagarkot is situated on the rim of the Kathmandu Valley about 15 kilometres (9 miles) north-east of Bhaktapur, and is served by tourist minibus from the capital and public bus from Bhaktapur. As with Dhulikhel, sunrise and sunset views of the mountains are magnificent, athough unlike Dhulikhel you can enjoy a classic panorama virtually from your hotel window. Of particular interest are those views of the Langtang and Jugal Himals, and Gauri Shankar, the beautiful twin-peaked mountain that dominates Rolwaling on the border with Tibet. Nagarkot also gives access to some pleasant low-level treks in hill country.

The Treks

Mountains should not be viewed from a car, they should not be traversed hurriedly; there is a kind of satisfaction that only effort and endurance can provide.
(George B. Schaller)

ROUTE SUMMARIES

LANGTANG

Langtang has not only the austere beauty of ice mountains accentuated by the friendly smile of flowery meadows alive with cattle - but it has the charm of reticence and the witchery of the unexpected. (H.W.Tilman)

Legendary mountain explorer Bill Tilman was the first Westerner to visit the Langtang Valley when, in the summer of 1949, he led a small expedition consisting of Peter Lloyd, Oleg Polunin, J.S. Scott and the Sherpa, Tenzing Norgay, to the Langtang, Ganesh and Jugal Himals.

Walking to the mountains from Kathmandu, the expedition followed the Trisuli Valley upstream as far as Syabrubensi, then bore eastward into Langtang where they spent several weeks exploring glaciers, passes and the valley itself before crossing into the Jugal Himal by what has since become known as Tilman's Pass. Tilman's account of this expedition is a classic of mountain-travel literature and is highly recommended reading for anyone planning a trek there. (*Nepal Himalaya*, now contained in the collection: *The Seven Mountain-Travel Books* published by Diadem/The Mountaineers, 1983.)

Tilman found Langtang to be "a fine, open valley, rich in flowers and grass, and flanked by great mountains." He wrote of it as a grazier's paradise, a sanctuary. He described magnificent peaks with graceful lines and made pithy comments about the state of some of the gompas visited during his comings and goings, and the villages in which he sometimes stayed. Despite his visit coinciding with the monsoon, and thus being denied much of the scenic grandeur by heavy clouds that brooded daily on the peaks, he made no attempt to conceal his enthusiasm for the valley and its walling mountains. Trekkers following in his wake will surely echo that enthusiasm and delight in what they find.

Although Tilman's party was the first from the West to enter Langtang (the Swiss, Toni Hagen, came next in 1952), the valley and its mountains had already been partially surveyed: "...the existing ¼-in. maps published by the Survey of India in 1931 are good only as far as they go," he wrote. "Good enough, that is, to destroy any illusions one might have of being an explorer."

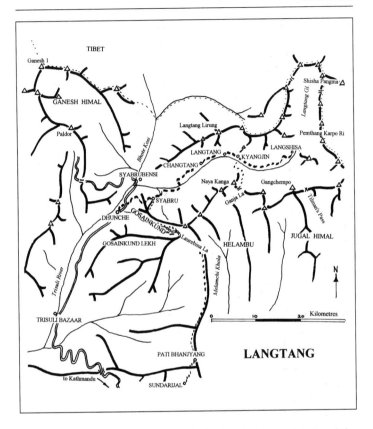

Long before even the main peaks had been triangulated and the general run of the valley defined by those unnamed surveyors, Langtang had been known to Tibetan Buddhists beyond the frontier as a *beyul*, or hidden, secret valley, a place to which a few would escape in times of trouble in order to keep Buddhism alive until it was safe to return to their homeland with the original teachings intact. During his visit Tilman learned via Tenzing that there was a tradition of a pass leading into Tibet at the head of the valley. Tenzing's informant, Nima Lama, insisted that neither he nor any living man had used it, for it had been closed at the time of the second Nepal-

Tibet war of 1854. Had that pass, one wonders, been one of the means of access for escaping Buddhists?

Signs of the Buddhist faith are evident throughout the valley, with numerous chortens, a handful of gompas (monasteries), great clusters of prayer flags, water-driven prayer wheels - and some of the longest mani walls to be found anywhere in the Himalaya. All of these structures hold great significance and should be passed on their left-hand side. To the uninitiated a *chorten* may appear to be just a pile of stones with maybe a few prayer flags sprouting from it. But this is, in fact, a stylized representation of the Buddha. A *stupa* is far more elaborately symbolic; its base denotes the solid earth, the dome above it represents water, while from each side of the rectangular tower above that, a pair of eyes gaze out over the four corners of the earth. Below the eyes, and often mistakenly assumed to be a nose, is the Sanskrit number one, painted there to underline the oneness of Buddha. Rising from the rectangular tower is a spire which may be either pyramidal or conical, and which is divided by 13 sections (the 13 steps to enlightenment), and finally, on top of all is a spike to symbolise the sacred light of Buddha. Upon *mani stones*, prayer flags and prayer wheels the words *Om Mani Padme Hum* (meaning: hail to the jewel in the lotus) are written countless times over. This great mantra, or prayer, is recited over and over again, being an important element in the meditative practice observed by followers of the Buddha. It is one more aspect of life in Langtang that adds to the trekker's journey.

Historically, the valley was regarded as a sanctuary within which no animal may be slaughtered, and the establishment in 1976 of the Langtang National Park has further reinforced this sanctuary ideal. Its name means 'to follow the yak' (*Lang* being Tibetan for 'yak'; *tang* - or more correctly, *dhang* - means 'to follow'), and there is a legend, again related by Tilman, that tells of a lama who went in search of his missing yak whose tracks led him into the valley. Imprints of the animal were left upon rocks at both Syabrubensi and Syarpagaon, but the lama didn't manage to catch his beast until it had led him far up the valley to Langshisa, where it promptly died. The lama skinned the yak there and then and spread the hide on a rock to dry. Unable to remove it, the skin is still there to this day, as witnessed by a reddish coloured rock.

Langtang is mostly inhabited by Tamangs, as is much of the Trisuli Valley region. These *Bhotiya* (Buddhist people of mountain Nepal) are among Nepal's most important hillfolk who, it is said, migrated from Tibet hundreds of years ago - those who live in Langtang village apparently came from the neighbourhood of Kyerong. They are predominantly Buddhist, have their own language, but maintain a tenuous link with Tibetan culture. Tilman found them "engagingly cheery". According to Tenzing their speech is similar to that of the inhabitants of Lachen, in northern Sikkim. Their houses are built of timber and stone and often roofed with shingles held down with flat stone slabs. In some villages lodges are typical Tamang homes that have been simply adapted to accommodate passing trekkers, which allows the visitor to observe the everyday life of these charming, hospitable people within their own four walls. Many Tamangs keep yaks and move them in a seasonal procession from one pasture (*kharka*) to the next, similar to the centuries-old practice of *transhumance* carried out in the European Alps. As a result there are several groups of low stone shelters (*goth* or *yersa*) used by herdsmen scattered throughout the valley. In Langtang village peasant farmers grow potatoes, barley and buckwheat, but some Tamangs also advertise their services as guides outside trailside lodges, while several trekking agencies based in Kathmandu employ Tamangs almost exclusively as cooks or sirdars.

*

The route into Langtang taken by the majority of trekkers today largely follows that pioneered by Tilman - except now that a rough road has been scored through the Trisuli Valley it is no longer necessary to walk all the way from Kathmandu. Instead it is usual to take a bus or hire a taxi as far as Dhunche, thus reducing the approach by four or five days, and begin the trek from there.

It would be possible to achieve a there-and-back Langtang trek in as little as a week from the roadhead at Dhunche, plus a day each way by bus or taxi from Kathmandu, but there is so much to see and to do, especially in the upper valley, that several extra days should be allowed. A number of suggestions for filling these days are given in the following pages.

From Dhunche a fairly easy day's trek leads through forest and across terraced hillsides to the village of Syabru, from where the Langtang Valley can be seen as a narrow wooded slice cutting through the northern mountain wall. Tilman and his party remained in the Trisuli Valley as far as Syabrubensi, and walked into Langtang from there along the true right bank of the Langtang Khola, but these days the standard route goes directly into the valley from Syabru and stays on the left bank through the lower reaches of the Langtang gorge before crossing a suspension bridge to the other side. It will take a day or so to trek through the gorge from Syabru, among forest nearly all the way, before the valley begins to open out. On occasion sneak previews of snow peaks towering over the valley are gained through the trees.

At Ghora Tabela there's a National Park checkpost situated beside the trail, where permit details must be entered in a book. From there the route is clear and obvious. Langtang becomes a classical U-shaped glacial valley which grows more beautiful as you progress through it. Beyond Langtang village, the largest in the valley, wonderful views of big mountains that wall the upper valley draw you on.

The lodges of Kyangjin Gompa are gained about four days from Dhunche. There's plenty to see and to do from a base there, but if you plan to explore much further upvalley you'll need to be self-sufficient with food and tent. Note that Langtang's only designated 'trekking peak', the 5846 metre (19,180ft) Naya Kanga, rises across the valley to the south of Kyangjin Gompa, with the Ganja La hinted just to its left (east).

*

The following trek is set out in day stages merely as a rough guide to aid planning. It is not intended that trekkers stick rigidly to this plan, for there are sufficient lodges along the way to enable independent travellers to stop whenever or wherever they feel appropriate. It would in any case be unfortunate if everyone adhered to the same itinerary, for in that way some lodges would quickly become crowded while others remained empty or even fell into disuse. Unless there's a very good reason for doing otherwise, please spread the load, thus

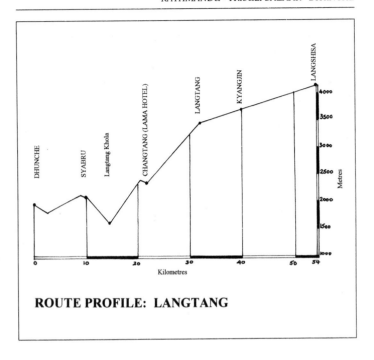

ROUTE PROFILE: LANGTANG

giving all the lodges an equal share of business. As approximate timings for the various stages are given, as well as a note of other villages and lodges available throughout, it should be possible to create your own itinerary from the information provided. Organised groups will have their own set timetable and overnight arrangements.

KATHMANDU - TRISULI BAZAAR - DHUNCHE

Distance:	112 kilometres (70 miles)
Time:	8-9 hours (or more)
Transport:	Bus or taxi
Accommodation:	Lodges in Trisuli Bazaar and Dhunche

The bus ride from Kathmandu to Dhunche may save several days of walking, but like most road journeys in Nepal, it is not made without sacrifice. Buses are uncomfortable, usually crowded, and painfully slow. The state of the road enforces the old adage 'more haste, less speed', for although the 72 kilometre (45 mile) stretch as far as Trisuli Bazaar has been surfaced, lack of maintenance has left it rutted, pot-holed and broken[1]. The remaining 40 kilometres (25 miles) leading to Dhunche are by dirt track[2] which climbs steeply in places along a narrow, sinuous route susceptible to landslide, particularly in the monsoon. It is, however, an interesting journey, made rather more comfortable if you hire a car instead of relying on the public bus.

* * *

The daily tourist bus to Dhunche leaves Kathmandu bus terminal at around 7.00am; tickets should be bought the day before. The route heads north-westward through Balaju before making a steady climb to the rim of the Kathmandu Valley, which is crossed at **KAKANI** (2066m: 6778ft). From the ridge at this point long views may be had to the Manaslu massif, with the Ganesh, Langtang and Jugal Himals forming the main focus of attention, while the broad trench of the Trisuli Valley[3] lies far below, being joined by that of the Tadi Khola flowing from the east.

On the way down to the valley the bus sometimes stops for refreshment at **RANIPAUWA**, the largest village en route to Dhunche, then continues twisting through terraced fields before crossing the Tadi Khola onto a plateau-like spit of land between that and the Trisuli River. Passing through flat, open fields of rice, millet and mustard, and past groups of houses shaded by banana trees, you then come to the ramshackle settlement of **TRISULI BAZAAR** (548m: 1798ft 4hrs or so, *accommodation, refreshments*)[4] one-time trail-head for treks to Langtang and Gosainkund. There is a police checkpoint here where trekking permits need to be shown.

Between Trisuli Bazaar and Dhunche the road remains on the east bank of the Trisuli River. At **BETRAWATI** (641m: 2103ft) a bridge takes the road across the Phalangu Khola, then begins a long twisting climb up a steep hillside, whereupon the track makes a brave attempt at following a contour that is broken by projecting spurs with the river a mere ribbon in places a thousand metres below. Views

upvalley show snow crowns tilted above converging ridges while small villages appear to hang among terraces on either side of the valley.

The old trek route followed a route well below the road, and passed through such villages as Bhotal, Mani Gaon and Ramche. The road now misses these completely and stays high. The bus stops only at various checkpoints on the way. Above Ramche there's a National Park checkpoint, and another just before reaching Dhunche, as well as police and military checks at various stages in between. It is certainly one of the most heavily-checked routes in Nepal, but happily once you begin trekking there are very few places where you'll need to show either your trekking permit or National Park entry permit.

DHUNCHE (1950m: 6398ft) is the administrative headquarters of Rasuwa District. Below the road it's quite an attractive village, but it holds little of appeal alongside the road itself where all the lodges and shops are situated. However, some of the lodges are above-average with regard to facilities, including electricity. From the village you gaze across the valley towards the Ganesh Himal where the summit tip of Paldor can be seen; or to a line of snowy peaks that stand beyond the frontier in Tibet, while Langtangs I and II and Langtang Lirung form a pristine crest high above the Langtang Valley.

Points of Interest Along the Way:

1: THE TRISULI ROAD was built in the mid-1960s in connection with a major hydro-electric scheme provided at Trisuli Bazaar by the Indian Technical Mission to supply Kathmandu with electricity.

2: THE TRISULI BAZAAR-DUNCHE ROAD at the time of writing has not been surfaced. As a consequence it is even more potholed than the Kathmandu-Trisuli road. Constructed in the 1980s, it continues beyond Dhunche to Syabrubensi at the mouth of the Langtang Valley, then crosses to the west bank of the Trisuli River (here known as the Bhote Kosi) where it twists up the hillside, eventually reaching a lead and zinc mine high in the Ganesh Himal. On occasion the road is cut by landslip. If motorised transport is trapped on the upvalley side, it is usually possible to transfer from one vehicle to another across the landslide.

3: THE TRISULI VALLEY has long been used as a route of trade between Kathmandu and Tibet, for there is no pass to cross from one country to the next since the river here rises on the Tibetan plateau and, like the Kali Gandaki which forms a moat between Dhaulagiri and Annapurna, flows through the great wall of the Himalaya. North of Dhunche the river is known as the Bhote Kosi and it only assumes its better-known name once it has been joined by the comparatively minor tributary of the Trisuli Khola that drains the Gosainkund lakes. For much of the way upstream of Betrawati the Trisuli Valley is narrow and steep-walled and is virtually a gorge beyond Syabrubensi, with the Ganesh Himal rising steeply to the west and summits of the Langtang peaks in excess of 6500 metres (21,325ft) being no more than 12 kilometres (7$^{1/}$2 miles) from the river to the east.

4: TRISULI BAZAAR is an unprepossessing little township just 30 kilometres (19 miles) from Kathmandu as the Himalayan crow flies, yet the road snakes for 72 kilometres (45 miles) over the mountains to reach it. Until the opening of the dirt road to Dhunche, Trisuli was the trail-head for Langtang treks. It remains of interest to trekkers, however, for the traditional cross-country route to Pokhara begins here, heading west initially through the lovely valley of the Sami Khola. Standing above Trisuli Bazaar to the east is Nuwakot, one-time fortress from which Prithvi Narayan Shah directed his campaign against the Kathmandu Valley in the mid-18th century.

DHUNCHE - BHARKHU - SYABRU

Distance:	10 kilometres (6 miles)
Time:	4 hours
Start altitude:	1950 metres (6398ft)
High point:	2300 metres (7546ft)
Height gain:	350 metres (1148ft)
Height loss:	172 metres (564ft)
Accommodation:	Lodges at Bharkhu and Syabru

The first stage of any trek is one of adjustment as you slowly come to terms with the landscape and the life of the countryside through which you travel. The stage that leads to Syabru is comparatively short and easy, with no great

altitude gains or losses, but it crosses ever-varied terrain, passes one or two small villages, looks down on others, enjoys forests of chir pine and rhododendron, and bright open hillsides with long views as a bonus. It's necessarily short because the next reasonable place to stop is too far away to reach comfortably on the first day. For that we may be thankful, for Syabru is not short of charm and with plenty of lodges and camp grounds to choose from.

After spending time in Kathmandu, then surviving a day's bus or car ride along the rough roads of Nepal, adjustment in the form of fresh air and exercise will no doubt be welcome. In the hill country there's a special fragrance to savour. The light too is different; bright and sharp with distances difficult to comprehend. And the sounds of village, farmland and forest may seem strange too at first - especially if this is your first time in the Himalaya.

Whether you're part of an organised group or trekking independently from lodge to lodge, there'll be a certain routine to your day. Most will want to start early. Village life begins soon after daybreak and lodge fires are often alight in readiness for breakfast long before seven. It's good to be on the trail by eight, even if it means finishing the day's trek early. There'll be tea-houses along the trail as a temptation to stop at regular intervals, either for just a cup of chaiyaa (tea), or for something more substantial to eat. There'll be views to photograph, villages to study, people to talk to. And if you arrive early at your chosen lodge or village camp ground, you'll not regret time spent exploring the neighbourhood.

* * *

To avoid wandering a pointless long loop in the road, descend from the lodges in Dhunche by a flight of stone steps that cuts away from the main street almost opposite Hotel Langtang View. These steps link various levels of the village. Halfway down bear right on a paved way between houses and eventually rejoin the road. From here Dhunche appears far more attractive than it had seemed from the main street.

Follow the road now as it winds round the terraced hillside on a steady descent to a bridge crossing the Trisuli Khola flowing from the south through a narrow gorge. (Note that it is this tributary that gives its name to the main valley river which, upstream of this point, is

known as the Bhote Kosi - the river from Tibet.) Across the sturdy bridge the road eases uphill against big grey looming cliffs, and with peaks of the Ganesh Himal on display across the valley.

About 45 minutes from Dhunche pass a row of low, simple buildings, one of which is a tea-house. Half an hour later enter **THULO BHARKHU** (1860m: 6102ft 1hr 15mins *accommodation, refreshments*), a pleasant little Tamang village astride the dirt road on a steep slope of hillside, and with good mountain views. There are three lodges here. The rest of the buildings are stone-walled houses with shingle roofs, most of which have a prayer flag beating the breezes from a tall pole.

Wander through the village, but a few metres beyond it leave the dirt road in favour of a path on the right which begins with a short flight of steps. The trail soon levels out, makes a contour round the hillside, then climbs a more extensive flight of stone steps with views back to Bharkhu set amid terraced slopes. About 30 minutes from Bharkhu pass a solitary tea-house. From here the path cuts up through forest, crosses a stream on a wooden footbridge and passes another tea-house. Then you emerge from the trees to fine views

The trail to Syabru provides a bird's-eye view onto the village of Mungra

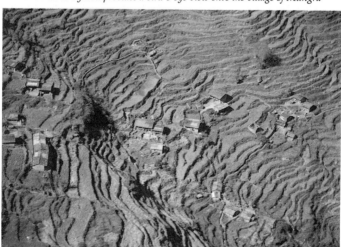

again of snowpeaks ahead, with a remarkable bird's-eye view onto the village of Mungra within abundant terraces steeply below. In about one hour from Bharkhu come to another tea-house on a wooded ridge (**NAWOR DANDA**; 1980m: 6496ft 2hrs 15mins).

The trail continues to climb, but with a few welcome level stretches, and comes to a high point with more fine views. It then crosses another stream on a wooden footbridge, followed by a steady hillside traverse which leads to the group of tea-houses of **BRABAL** (2200m: 7218ft 3hrs *refreshments*).

Two minutes beyond Brabal the trail forks. Take the upper path and moments later look down on the newly-built Shedup Cheling Gompa. The route now follows a comfortable contour. Across the valley Paldor[1] and other eastern peaks of the Ganesh Himal display their summit snows, while the hamlets of Gri and Shipa cling to gorge-like walls high above the river. Curving round a spur at the high point of 2300 metres (7546ft), where there's a small chorten, Syabru and the Langtang Valley come into view ahead. The village traces the rim of a tree-lined spur with the narrow, tightly-cleft lower end of the Langtang Valley beyond it. The trail slopes down, fairly steeply at times, passes more chortens, and enters the top end of **SYABRU** in a little under an hour from Brabal.

SYABRU (2118m: 6949ft) has several camp grounds and a good many lodges, nearly all of which are found at the upper end of the village with their yellow name-boards prominently displayed. It's not unusual for trekkers to be met on the approach trail by lodge representatives touting for business. Syabru also has a small gompa, a school, a Nepalese Army post, and a few shops selling basic goods. A speciality here is the weaving of brightly coloured belts; colourful knitted socks are also on sale.

The lower part of the village, without a plethora of lodge name-boards, is more attractive than the more blatantly commercial upper section. The rooftop of each house overlaps that of the one next door as they slope down the narrow ridge crest. Rarely is the crest broad enough to allow two buildings to be built side by side upon it. Prayer flags rise from practically every house, many of which have beautifully carved windows, while a vast array of terraced fields of millet, maize and wheat curve round the agricultural basin overlooked by the village.

Sculpture preparations for a festival at Syabru's gompa

Points of Interest Along the Way:

1: PALDOR stands at the south-eastern limit of the Ganesh Himal, and is a very popular 'trekking peak' of 5928 metres (19,449ft). First climbed by Bill Tilman, Peter Lloyd, Tenzing Norgay and Da Namgyal in 1949, it is approached by way of the dirt road serving the lead and zinc mines at Somdang. Bill O'Connor's book *The Trekking Peaks of Nepal* suggests four routes on this mountain, together with information about several smaller peaks in the neighbourhood. Note that 'trekking peaks' are not quite what their title suggests, and should not be considered lightly. Mountaineering skills and equipment are required to tackle them.

SYABRU - CHANGTANG (LAMA HOTEL)

Distance:	12 kilometres (7$^{1/2}$ miles)
Time:	4$^{1/2}$ hours
Start altitude:	2118 metres (6949ft)
High point:	Ganesh View Hotel (2385m: 7825ft)
Low point:	1661 metres (5449ft)
Height gain:	774 metres (2539ft)
Height loss:	527 metres (1729ft)
Accommodation:	Several lodges spaced along the route, mostly quite basic.

Trails change. Once-important routes become virtually obsolete for one reason or another, while replacement paths are created that soon become well-established, as on this stage of the trek. Some maps still show a high route leading south-east then eastward from Syabru, before swinging north to descend to the Langtang Khola at a bridge which takes the trail across to the north bank, while the present route is not indicated at all. The main route followed by about 95% of trekkers on this stage, however, enters the Langtang Valley proper at its narrow, gorge-like western end, some way downstream of the old trail. It's clear on the ground, although there is a short stretch where the path picks a way across a huge landslide that occurred in the 1987 monsoon and has yet to become stabilised by vegetation.

For much of the way through the gorge the trail climbs and falls in luxuriant mixed forest. At certain times of year this is alive with birdsong. Langur monkeys may be seen, and it is claimed that the red panda and wild boar also inhabit this part of the valley. Although there is no proper village settlement on this stage, there are plenty of somewhat basic lodges that provide alternative accommodation on both sides of the river.

*   *   *

Leaving Syabru's hotels descend through the remaining village, then veer right on a clear trail that cuts round among terraced fields, passing a few scattered houses and an occasional lodge. Groups sometimes camp here when the harvest has been taken. The way slopes down among bamboo thickets into the indented hillside sliced

81

by the Ghopche Khola which is crossed on a steel bridge (1943m: 6375ft 30mins) - note the watermill just below the bridge. On the far side the trail climbs, then eases along the hillside with views of the Ganesh peaks to the north-west framed by trees. Syabru can also be clearly seen stubbed along its ridge crest.

About 45 minutes from Syabru pass a solitary tea-house, and another very simple place five minutes later built on the nose of a hillside spur - perfectly situated for trekkers returning from Langtang, for it stands at the top of a long and wearisome climb. The trail now begins its descent to the river, much of the way through tall, view-screening bamboo. In places it is narrow and quite steep, and after rain the path can become rather slippery. Approaching the landslide area the trail to Syabrubensi, not passable during the monsoon, cuts off to the left. Ignore this, cross the landslide and finish descending to the low point of this stage where there are hot springs in the bed of the valley near the river (1661m: 5449ft 1hr 20mins).

Rising now beside the river in five minutes the path brings you to two small *bhatti*. Beyond these the trail makes a steady climb in forest on the south bank, twisting to and fro as elevation is gained through the gorge-like narrows. Eventually the gradient eases and again the path brings you close to the Langtang Khola, which here boils and thrashes its way between great water-smoothed boulders. In another five minutes come to **Bamboo Lodge** (2hrs 20mins *accommodation, refreshments*) set in a forest clearing. Despite its name the lodge is not made of bamboo at all, but is a sturdy little hotel of stone construction.

Continue uphill through the jungly forest for a further half-hour or so, when you reach a suspension bridge. Basic lodges guard both sides of the river; **Langtang Khola Bridge Lodge** and **Namaste Tibet Lodge** (2042m: 6699ft 3hrs *accommodation, refreshments*). The first is on the cool, shady side, the other is more substantial and catches filtered sunshine, while the river thunders between them over a series of rapids. Cross the bridge to the north bank.

This side of the valley is not so densely forested, and is generally much more warm and dry than the south bank. Once more the trail climbs through the wooded gorge (prickly-leaved oak and rhododendron), and about 40 minutes from the bridge comes to **Langtang View Hotel**. Continue to the day's high point, the aptly-named **Ganesh View Hotel** (2385m: 7825ft 4hrs *accommodation,*

refreshments) where there's a trail junction. The left-hand path is the high route to/from Syabrubensi via Syarpagaon, which makes an alternative descent route. Continue ahead, now losing height for a further 20 minutes or so, to reach the collection of basic, stone-built lodges of Changtang.

CHANGTANG (2365m: 7759ft), more popularly known as **LAMA HOTEL**, is set in a forest clearing near the river. There are several lodges, unsophisticated but pleasant enough, and camping spaces for one or two groups. Some of the lodges, owned by villagers from Syarpagaon, are open throughout the year.

CHANGTANG (LAMA HOTEL) - LANGTANG VILLAGE

Distance:	10 kilometres (6 miles)
Time:	4-4^1/$_2$ hours
Start altitude:	2365 metres (7759ft)
High point:	Langtang (3500m: 11,483ft)
Height gain:	1135 metres (3724ft)
Accommodation:	Lodges at Gumnachowk, Ghora Tabela, Thangsep and Langtang

This stage makes a fine trekking day. It may be yet another short one, but there's sufficient increase in altitude to affect some trekkers who are slow to acclimatise, and it would be foolhardy to press on beyond Langtang village if you'd spent the previous night in Changtang. Remain alert for signs of AMS in yourself and your companions, and monitor any symptoms that occur.

Beyond Changtang the valley remains narrow, V-shaped and river-carved, but once the forest is left behind at Ghora Tabela teasing views of mountains ahead give promise for the days to come. Now you will notice how the upper part of the valley has a classic U-shape to it, as if to underline the fact that it had once been scoured by glaciers, and can sense the presence of big mountains that have yet to reveal their full majesty.

* * *

From Lama Hotel's clearing the trail climbs on into forest again, in places quite steeply. Although views are restricted, the great tatters of Spanish moss hanging from the trees, the mossy banks, and ferns that congregate on damp trailside boulders and the delicate orchids that grow there all help create an exotic atmosphere. Birdsong and the occasional clatter of monkeys add to the splendours of this forest.

After about 35 minutes the trail brings you level with a massive landslide on the opposite bank, and there ahead is a tantalising view of Langtang peaks apparently blocking the valley. The way continues stuttering along the valley, climbing here and there, and in an hour from Lama Hotel comes to **GUMNACHOWK**, with the Riverside Hotel and, seven minutes later, Woodlands Hotel set in a clearing. One hour later arrive at **GHORA TABELA** (2880m: 9449ft 2hrs *accommodation, refreshments*)[1] and the stone-built Hotel Tibetan. Just a few minutes beyond the lodge stands a National Park checkpoint where permits need to be shown. A Nepalese Army post is situated to the rear of this.

Rhododendron and berberis add colour to the scene as you continue upvalley. For a while the path remains fairly constant, but

Lodge-owner and his family at Thangsep

then a steepish pull brings you to an upper section of valley. The trail zig-zags higher and higher, and at the top of the rise brings you to **THANGSEP** (2hrs 35mins) with two small lodges. Still rising in steps interrupted by pleasant level sections dotted with *goths*, or temporary shelters, the valley broadens and curves ahead. Fifteen minutes beyond Thangsep pass another tea-house, and 45 minutes later come to Langtang Mountain View and Lodge, which has views to Langtang village. Above the lodge will be seen Langtang's gompa[(2)] and a forest of prayer flags.

Losing height now the way is funnelled between drystone walls that lead to the edge of the village, then past several watermills and a water-driven prayer wheel into Langtang itself where sections of mani wall divide the pathway through.

LANGTANG (3500m: 11,483ft) is the largest village in the valley; a scattered community of flat-roofed, stone-built houses and lodges set among broad yak pastures and large walled fields of buckwheat, barley and potatoes. The upper part of the village is a close gathering of houses, some of which have neat carvings round their windows; most have small courtyards in which yaks, hens, sheep and goats are

Typical Tamang house in Langtang village

contained. Dating from 1949 Tilman's description remains good today: It was then, he said, "a settlement of some thirty families rich in cows, yaks and sheep". Yaks may well be seen here today, but there are also many *zhoms* (or *dzums*) - a yak-cow hybrid which gives more milk than either a yak or a cow (the hybrid male, the *dzopkyo*, is infertile and is used either for load-carrying or ploughing).

Points of Interest Along the Way:

1: GHORA TABELA means 'horse stable', and is so named because, according to Harka Gurung's *Vignettes of Nepal*, at one time it was the site of a government horse farm. Tibetan refugees were also once housed there, in buildings now used as the National Park checkpoint and by the Army.

2: LANGTANG GOMPA is worth a visit. Enquire at one of the lodges on the hill just below for information about access. In 1949 Bill Tilman was shown over the monastery by the resident lama, and his description of the contents makes interesting reading.

LANGTANG VILLAGE - KYANGJIN GOMPA

Distance:	9 kilometres (5$^{1}/_{2}$ miles)
Time:	2$^{1}/_{2}$-3 hours
Start altitude:	3500 metres (11,483ft)
High point:	Kyangjin Gompa (3749m: 12,300ft)
Height gain:	249 metres (817ft)
Accommodation:	Lodges below Muna, at Singdum and Kyangjin Gompa

A delightful morning's walk leads from Langtang to Kyangjin, through charming mountain scenery that will demand plenty of photographic halts. On the way the trail passes numerous mani walls, among them, some of the longest in all Nepal. As for mountains, the prize on this stage is the glorious ice-fluted Gangchempo (6387m: 20,955ft) which beckons from its guardian position on the south side of the valley way beyond Kyangjin Gompa.

*   *   *

The trail leads through Langtang village and across yak pastures damp with meandering streams and small pools, before rising up an old moraine topped by a pair of large chortens from which a fine view is had back down to the village. A series of mani walls now leads the route upvalley (remember to keep on the left-hand side of both mani walls and chortens) with Gangchempo forming a prominent landmark to the east.

At the end of the mani walls descend into a small stream bed, and up the other side to yet more mani walls where the valley is broad and open. In about 35 minutes from Langtang pass the hamlet of Muna off to the left, and five minutes later come to one or two small lodges.

The valley becomes exceedingly beautiful in its wild, untamed way, and fine views accompany every stride. The path remains on the north side of the glacial torrent, and climbs each natural valley step without demanding too much effort. In autumn the tan and scarlet colours of wayside shrubs and the cropped, sunburnt grasses are most attractive and reminiscent of the Khumbu region near Namche Bazaar.

SINGDUM (1hr 45mins *accommodation, refreshments*) has a couple of simple lodges, and beyond these you continue to gain altitude in

Between Langtang and Kyangjin the splendours of the valley become apparent

Kyangjin Gompa, a simple white building flanked by big mountains

modest steps, then cross a wooden bridge over a stream draining from the Lirung Glacier which empties into a corrie above to the left, where more peaks begin to show themselves.

The way climbs onto moraines pushed down by the retreating glacier, and topping a rise you look onto Kyangjin Gompa with its cluster of prayer flags and chortens set immediately below the glacial amphitheatre dominated by Langtang Lirung[1]. Follow a last twist in the trail and there, huddled against the moraine spur on which you stand, are the lodges and cheese factory of Kyangjin, with a broad open pasture stretching ahead. Mountain views are quite spectacular.

KYANGJIN GOMPA (3749m: 12,300ft), with its several lodges and camping grounds, offers the highest accommodation for trekkers in the valley. Originally used as a summer grazing settlement of low stone huts in view of the gompa's protection, it was visited by Toni Hagen in 1952 (three years after Tilman), whose reports inspired a further visit by Werner Schulthess, a Swiss agricultural adviser to the United Nations. It was Schulthess who established the cheese factory there in 1955, the first in Nepal. Today the factory produces some 7000kg (15,500lbs) of hard cheese each year from the herds of yaks

and zhoms that graze the valley pastures. The factory is worth a visit, especially if you intend buying some of the cheese. As for the gompa which overlooks the lodges, this is no longer open for inspection, and there's just a single monk living there.

The southern wall of the valley is very fine, and as the valley itself is quite broad the peaks are not badly foreshortened. Of particular interest is the 'trekking peak' of Naya Kanga[2] which looms above Kyangjin to the south-south-west, with the hinted Ganja La to its left as you face it. A long crest runs eastward from the Ganja La towards Gangchempo, while the valley's northern wall shows a less dramatic profile. However, this northern side has several accessible summits from which more staggering scenery is unravelled.

Points of Interest Along the Way:

1: LANGTANG LIRUNG (7245m: 23,770ft) is the highest of the Langtang mountains, a dramatic peak whose huge south-east face soars above the glacial cirque immediately behind Kyangjin Gompa. Several tragedies occurred during early attempts to climb the mountain; in 1961 two Japanese climbers, Morimoto and Oshima, were killed along with Sherpa Gyaltsen Norbu when an avalanche overwhelmed them, and two Italians lost their lives during an expedition in 1963. In 1964 an Australian attempt was beaten back by bad weather, but the mountain was finally climbed in 1978 by a joint Japanese/Nepali team.

2: NAYA KANGA (5846m: 19,180ft), formerly called Ganja La Chuli, is the only scheduled 'trekking peak' in the Langtang Himal. It's a handsome looking mountain when viewed from Kyanjin, alpine in character, hung about with small glaciers and with a variety of rock ribs dividing its main features. It is not known who made the first ascent. Bill O'Connor's guide to *The Trekking Peaks of Nepal* suggests a route on the north-east face as the voie normale, but a change in the upper glacier has altered this route slightly. Note that the designation of a mountain as a 'trekking peak' does not imply that any fit walker could simply walk up it. Mountaineering skills and equipment will definitely be required to tackle Naya Kanga. 'Trekking peaks' in Nepal are selected mountains for which a minimum of bureaucracy needs to be faced before permission is given to climb them. O'Connor's book gives details.

TIME IN KYANGJIN

He who knows not whither to go is in no hurry to move.
(H.W.Tilman)

Unless you are really pushed for time, it would be worth spending a few days exploring the neighbourhood of Kyangjin Gompa from where there's no shortage of walks and easy summits to reach. The following suggestions merely hint at the range of possibilities.

The Lirung Amphitheatre

Immediately behind the gompa a huge cirque, or amphitheatre, has been carved out by glaciers spilling from Langtang Lirung (7245m: 23,770ft), Kimshun (6745m: 22,129ft) and Yansa Tsenji (6575m: 21,572ft). The Lirung Glacier is the only one of any great substance left now, and it still noses its way from the inner sanctuary, bulldozing moraine heaps towards the valley floor.

An interesting half-day walk may be spent wandering up the moraines into the sanctuary of the Lirung amphitheatre where a wild scene of soaring rock walls and hanging glaciers will reward your efforts. It's a good way to aid acclimatisation, and could be achieved on the day of arrival at Kyangjin Gompa. But choose settled weather and good visibility, for the route could be somewhat tricky to find in thick mist.

From the lodges go up to the gompa and continue above it on a thin trail that climbs towards the glacial amphitheatre. Although the trail is narrow it is quite clear in reasonable visibility, but it has a few alternatives cutting from it. Just continue heading up towards the amphitheatre's opening, keeping to the right of the torrent which drains it. Eventually top a moraine crest which provides direct views of hanging glaciers and challenging walls that curve around you. There are also good views behind to the south where Naya Kanga dominates. (About 1^{1}/₂-2hrs up, ^{1}/₂hr down.)

Minor Peak North of Kyangjin

Mistakenly called Kyangjin Ri by some trekkers, the minor peak rising directly above the lodges and clearly marked with a cluster of

prayer flags is a tremendous viewpoint, reached in about an hour and a half. The way is by a very steep path, not technically difficult, but it cannot be recommended for anyone with a poor head for heights.

From the lodges a variety of trails rise up the lower southern face of the hill cutting back and forth, but these steadily converge and slant a little to the right (east), climbing steeply to come onto the narrow ridge a few paces to the north-east of the actual summit. Further north another summit crest of prayer flags may be seen - this is the true Kyangjin Ri whose ascent is described below. From the crown of our minor peak Langtang Lirung looks quite magnificent, as does Naya Kanga. The route to the Ganja La is clearly visible too, and there's a wonderful bird's-eye view directly onto the lodge roofs below. (1-1¹/₂hrs up, ¹/₂hr down.)

Kyangjin Ri

Kyangjin Ri (4773m: 15,659ft) is unseen from the lodges, hidden behind the minor peak described above. It's another easily reached summit by a route that follows a long grassy gully to a narrow ridge crest overlooking the Lirung amphitheatre. Views from the top are

Broad-topped Kimshun, photographed from Kyangjin Ri

even better than those from the minor neighbouring peak; a vast array of peaks, ridges and hinted valleys spread out in a 360 degree panorama.

Before setting out study the weather conditions and carry some food and liquid refreshment with you.

Wander up to the lower, southern flank of the minor peak directly above the lodges, and take one of the many paths that slant across the face. Do not climb too high, but follow a trail easing eastwards (right) across the lower face, then cutting into a grassy seam of a gully between Kyangjin Ri and the next minor peak to the right. Follow a narrow path that climbs through this gully, near the head of which it opens to a broad hillside rich in alpine flowers. Cairns guide the route here.

Come onto a long saddle from which you gain spectacular views into the glacial amphitheatre which plunges at your feet. Across it rises Kimshun with its hanging glacier. Bear left and wander along the narrow ridge, cutting below its left-hand side in places, and gain the flag-festooned summit about two hours or so from Kyangjin. The stunning south-east face of Langtang Lirung is on show, but the whole sweep of ridge and peak that lines the amphitheatre is worth studying. On the opposite side of the Langtang Valley the great wall of peaks that separates Langtang from Helambu invites inspection, while far off the summit tips of numerous mountains fuss each distant horizon. (2-2$^{1}/_{2}$hrs up, 1-1$^{1}/_{2}$hrs down.)

The easiest way back to Kyangjin is to reverse the route of ascent. However, an alternative is to go down the ridge heading roughly south-west to gain the summit of the minor peak whose prayer flags are clearly seen below. Caution is advised if you do this, however, for the ridge is very steep and one slip could prove fatal. Keep away from the right-hand edge too, as this is crumbling. From the minor peak descend a clear twisting path down the face of the mountain to the lodges which will be on view all the way from the secondary summit.

Yala

The summer grazing hamlet of Yala lies in a remote pasture to the east of, and about 900 metres (3000ft) higher than, Kyangjin and can be reached by a reasonably clear trail in about 3$^{1}/_{2}$ hours. Yala also has a small cheese-making facility, and enjoys very fine views to the

Ganja La. Food and plenty of drink must be carried.

Leave Kyangjin on the upvalley trail, and about ten minutes from the lodges depart from the main trail on a secondary path on the left that contours the hillside to the north. After about an hour you come to a few stone shelters. The way continues, rising steadily to another *kharka* (yak pasture) at about 4150 metres (13,615ft). From here the trail rounds a spur and climbs to a ridge (4389m: 14,340ft) about 2¹/₂ hours from Kyangjin. Head north alongside a stream and you will reach the huts of Yala (4633m: 15,200ft). (3¹/₂hrs up, about 2hrs back.)

From Yala the grassy, flag-adorned summit of **Yala Peak** (4984m: 16,352ft) - an excellent viewpoint - is easily reached in two hours. (This Yala Peak should not be confused with another Yala Peak of about 5500 metres a little further east; that has a glacier and requires mountaineering skills to climb, and is usually tackled from Nubamatang.)

Nubamatang

Upvalley from Kyangjin, on the way to Langshisa Kharka, one or two small yak herders' settlements occupy idyllic sites with truly magical views. Nubamatang is one such; a few stone huts on a grassy shelf above the north bank of the Langtang Khola, with the huge snow dome of Pemthang Karpo Ri and more shapely Langshisa Ri forming a backdrop to the east.

While the site of Nubamatang is delightful, it is the 2¹/₂-3 hour walk to it that makes this outing so worthwhile. As you progress through the valley, so one mountain after another shows itself and draws you on into wonderland. "A gentle but continuous bend tantalizes its admirers," said Tilman when he first trekked here, "draws them on impatiently to see beyond the next corner, maintaining for them the thrill of discovery almost to the end".

A description of the route will be found in the following section under the heading: 'Kyangjin Gompa - Nubamatang - Langshisa Kharka', but is outlined separately here in order to draw it to the attention of trekkers who are unable to proceed as far as Langshisa for lack of camping equipment. By walking to Nubamatang and back a splendid day's trekking can be achieved. It would be possible to make it to Langshisa and back in a day, but that would be a bit of a push. The route to Nubamatang is every bit as rewarding as the full

stage to Langshisa. (Allow 2¹/₂-3hrs up, 2hrs back.)

Make sure you have enough food and liquid refreshment with you for the day, and plenty of film for your camera.

KYANGJIN GOMPA - NUBAMATANG - LANGSHISA KHARKA

Distance:	13 kilometres (8 miles)
Time:	4-4¹/₂ hours
Start altitude:	3749 metres (12,300ft)
High point:	Langshisa (4084m: 13,399ft)
Height gain:	335 metres (1099ft)
Accommodation:	None

This is probably the finest day's walk to be had in the Langtang Valley, for between Kyangjin and Langshisa the trail leads through an avenue of superb mountains, and with more fine peaks ahead to lure you on. Apart from the crossing of a glacial torrent just beyond Kyangjin where ice-glazed rocks could cause difficulties in the early morning, there are no problems; the route is straightforward with very few steep inclines to tackle.

The high mountain scenery in this part of the valley has a justifiable reputation for grandeur, and although the landscape around Kyangjin will satisfy all who see it, it is merely a tease when compared to that of the upper reaches towards the kharkas of Jatang and Nubamatang.

Camping equipment, cooking fuel and food will have to be carried beyond Kyangjin as there are neither lodges nor tea-houses. There are, however, plenty of natural campsites throughout the valley. When camping please make absolutely certain that you leave no rubbish behind, and that latrine pits are sited well away from water sources, and are adequately covered afterwards.

*   *   *

Leaving the lodges of Kyangjin behind, follow a narrow but clear trail upvalley. After about 20 minutes cross a stream flowing through an alluvial fan (caution advised when the rocks by which you cross are glazed, or later in the day when the water level may be high), and

The trail from Kyangjin to Langshisa Kharka follows the north bank of the Langtang Khola

slope down into the broad pastures beyond. Pass alongside the STOL airstrip (45 minutes), beyond which the valley narrows and curves gently to the left, with Gangchempo[1] soaring above on the south bank of the river a short distance away upstream.

The trail then rises easily above the river, remaining always on the true right bank (north shore) of the Langtang Khola. The path is clear, undulating but undemanding; at one point it squeezes through a cleft in a boulder, tiny edelweiss and occasional gentians flower in November beside the trail, and the valley retains its magic every step of the way.

Come to the *kharka* of **JATANG** (c.3810m: 12,500ft 1¹/₂hrs), which consists of half a dozen or so stone huts on a grassy shelf; an attractive site with Langshisa Ri (6310m: 20,702ft) dominating the view ahead. Now hillside spurs are rounded to open a clear view upvalley. Gangchempo becomes foreshortened off to the right, but Langshisa Ri and its snow-dome neighbour, Pemthang Karpo Ri[2], grow in stature as you progress towards them.

The path slopes down to river level, then begins to rise again. A little over an hour from Jatang you will come to the five stone huts of

View downstream from Nubamatang

NUBAMATANG (c.4000m: 13,123ft 2¹/₂hrs), tucked against the hillside high above the river. Just ahead a huge wall of lateral moraine shielding the West Langtang (or Shalbachum) Glacier appears to block the valley.

Between the *kharka* and the moraine wall the trail passes a small tarn, then drops into a marshy pasture. Unless you wish to view a scene of glacial debris, converging moraines, grey pools and streams and the wild upper reaches of the valley, do not be tempted onto the moraine wall. (However, there are a few cairns to guide you if you fancy the additional exercise - it will take nearly an hour to reach the top from here.)

The Langshisa trail grows thin, but should you lose it, simply aim for the southern (right-hand) end of the lateral moraine and you should soon find the continuing path. It leads through much vegetation, crosses several streams (some on stepping stones, two on log bridges) round the moraine snout where a vast chunk has collapsed, then climbs up to the original path that was cut by landslip.

Langshisa Ri and Pemthang Karpo Ri appear to block the head of the valley

The trail to Laurebinayak provides spectacular views of Langtang Lirung
Laurebinayak is a cold and windy spot, but it enjoys magnificent views

Jatang kharka and Gangchempo

Turning the moraine spur the Langtang Glacier appears ahead, stretching off towards Tibet. Above to the right is Langshisa Ri with the Langshisa Glacier flowing down beside it. The trail then eases down to the scrubby yak pasture and lone hut of **LANGSHISA KHARKA** (4084m: 13,399ft), reached about one hour from Nubamatang.

Points of Interest Along the Way:

1: GANGCHEMPO (6387m: 20,955ft) is a graceful mountain suitably named Fluted Peak by Tilman on account of the long ribs of ice that streak its western face. Seen on the walk upvalley from Kyangjin it stands alone, "smiling down upon the valley with a face of glistening purity framed between clean-cut snow ridges of slender symmetry". Tilman and Lloyd failed in their attempt to climb it during the monsoon of 1949. It is believed to have been climbed unofficially 'alpine style' in 1971 by two Americans.

2: PEMTHANG KARPO RI (6830m: 22,408ft), sometimes known as Dome Blanc, straddles the frontier between Nepal and Tibet. A huge mountain, it was first climbed by a Swiss expedition under the leadership of Raymond Lambert in 1955.

BEYOND LANGSHISA

From a camp at Langshisa Kharka below the impressive Morimoto Peak (6750m: 22,146ft) exploration of the wild and uncompromising upper reaches of the valley becomes possible. But wherever you go beyond Langshisa it is essential to proceed with caution as this is remote country and it is quite possible that you won't see any other trekkers. Even a modest accident here could have serious consequences.

Langtang Glacier

The Langtang Glacier curves northward, a rubble-covered highway of ice, approximately 17 kilometres (10$^{1}/_{2}$ miles) long, that begins high up near the Tibetan border a little west of the massive Shisha

Pangma (8046m: 26,398ft - also known as Xixabangma or Gosainthan), last of the eight thousanders to be climbed. Tilman and Lloyd searched the upper glacier for a pass into Tibet and produced a not-altogether accurate map of the region. Three years later, in 1952, Toni Hagen made extensive explorations here and discovered a col just north of Goldum. A trail of sorts goes up the ablation valley to the left of the glacier, passing another stone hut, but it later becomes necessary to go onto the moraine and then the glacier itself to make further progress. Needless to say, the scenery is spectacular.

Langshisa Glacier

Opposite Langshisa Kharka to the south the Langshisa Glacier flows between Langshisa Ri and Gangchempo, its trough curving eastwards with a glorious amphitheatre of peaks at its head. Among this sweep of mountains stands the handsome 'prince' of the Jugal Himal, Dorje Lakpa (6990m: 22,933ft), with the higher Lenpo Gang (Big White Peak 7083m: 23,238ft) on the Tibetan border nearby. (Nepalese territory projects northward like a finger into Tibet at the head of the Langtang Valley.)

It is possible to cross into the Langshisa glen by way of a wooden bridge (not always there!) over the Langtang Khola a short distance upstream of Langshisa Kharka. The route to Tilman's Pass travels this way, and mountaineering skills will be required to make progress over it.

WAYS OUT

The choice of route to take out of the Langtang Valley depends very much on your plans for the next few days, on the amount of time at your disposal, mode of trekking and mountaineering abilities. Options available may be summarised as below:

1: **Crossing Tilman's Pass** (5304m: 17,402ft) from Langshisa Kharka and descent through the Jugal Himal, or via the lakes of Panch Pokhari into Helambu.

2: **Crossing the Ganja La** (5200m: 17,060ft) south of Kyangjin Gompa, and descent through Helambu via Tarke Ghyang.

3:   **Return down-valley to Syabrubensi**, cutting away from the main trail just beyond Changtang (Lama Hotel) on a high path along the northern hillside to Syarpagaon and Syabrubensi, there to take the road route back to Kathmandu.

4:   **Back-track through the Langtang Valley to Syabru** (with an option to break away on a climb to Gosainkund and Helambu) or on to Dhunche for a return to Kathmandu.

Both Tilman's Pass and the Ganja La crossings call for a degree of mountaineering skill. A guide who knows the way is usually necessary for both, plus camping equipment and food for several days. The two routes that return down-valley are straightforward, and are supplied with plenty of lodges.

Tilman's Pass

This route is a serious undertaking. Full mountaineering equipment (ropes, ice axes, crampons) will be required, as will tents, food and cooking fuel for 9-10 days beyond Kyangjin. From **LANGSHISA KHARKA** the way heads up alongside the Langshisa Glacier, and over the great moraines before climbing up towards the pass, which is found between Gangchempo and Urkinmang. The pass is not always easy to reach, and on the southern side the Balephi Glacier has convex slopes that conceal a dangerous icefall. Once down off the ice there's a choice of either working a sometimes difficult route down the flank of the **BALEPHI KHOLA VALLEY** which drains the Jugal Himal, or of taking a high trail south-westward to the lakes of **PANCH POKHARI** and crossing into Helambu. (Bill O'Connor's *Adventure Treks - Nepal* provides an account of this crossing as, of course, does Tilman's *Nepal Himalaya*.)

Ganja La

Although it is less serious than Tilman's Pass, the Ganja La crossing is not to be tackled lightly. Good, settled weather conditions are needed, as is mountaineering experience. It is usually impassable in winter. As there is no accommodation for several days, a tent plus food and cooking fuel will be needed. It may be possible to hire a guide who knows the route at one of the lodges in the Langtang Valley.

The approach to the pass begins at Kyangjin. A short first day is usually taken to gain the yak pasture of **NGEGANG** (c.4000m: 13,123ft) on the slopes of Naya Kanga, although some trekkers who are well-acclimatised and fit make an early start and camp (in good conditions only) up by the pass itself. The snow-covered Ganja La is crossed at 5200 metres (17,060ft), the saddle marked by a large cairn and a cluster of prayer flags overlooked by the east face of Naya Kanga.

Descent to Helambu begins with shifting screes, then snow, before coming to a large basin and a trail of sorts which leads to the valley of the **YANGRI KHOLA**. From a camp at about 4200 metres (13,780ft) it will take another two days to reach the busy Sherpa village of **TARKE GHYANG**. Thereafter Helambu has plenty of lodges and tea-houses, and it will take just two or three days to reach Kathmandu.

The Trail to Syabrubensi

Trekkers who need to make a fairly direct return to Kathmandu should consider varying their upvalley route by taking the high trail alternative from a little south of Changtang (Lama Hotel). This trail was the original route into the Langtang Valley. It provides very different views to those of the lower option, visits two or three more villages and gives an opportunity to catch the bus back to Kathmandu without walking on to Dhunche. Lodges in Syabrubensi are somewhat basic - allow two full days from Kyangjin.

The route is as follows. Take the main trail down-valley from Kyangjin to **CHANGTANG**. Just beyond Lama Hotel the path climbs to a high point with a lodge (Ganesh View Hotel) and a trail junction. There is a signpost pointing to 'Sherpa Village'. Take this upper path which leads to **SYARPAGAON** (2507m: 8225ft). Beyond the village the trail continues high above the valley, sometimes climbing, sometimes following a contour until rounding a spur you come to a forest above the main Trisuli (or Bhote Kosi) Valley. Here you begin to descend to **KHANGJUNG** (2210m: 7251ft 2½-3hrs from Syarpagaon) - shown as Kakdinma on some maps. There's a trail junction by a mani wall where you take the left-hand option and descend steeply through terraces to a pine forest and come to **MANGAL** (1494m: 4902ft). Now follow a trail south for half an hour

to reach **SYABRUBENSI** (1417m: 4649ft 1$^{1}/_{2}$hrs from Khangjung) and the dirt road to Trisuli and Kathmandu. Syabrubensi is the site of a Tibetan refugee settlement; there are hot springs nearby on the opposite side of the Bhote Kosi.

The Trail to Syabru

This route merely reverses the trail already described. It will take two days to reach Syabru from Kyangjin, and a further day to Dhunche; so allow four days to travel from Kyangjin to Kathmandu.

Trekkers who wish to visit the sacred lakes of Gosainkund, and maybe continue on to Helambu, are referred to the next section: 'Gosainkund'.

Hindu tradition has it that long ago the gods were churning an ocean from which they hoped to find the waters of immortality. From the depths there arose poison, and fearing that lurking demons might use it against them, it was drunk by Shiva whose throat turned blue. In pain and with a raging thirst Shiva hastened to the cool snows of the mountains where he thrust his trident (*trisul*) into the hillside. At once three springs of pure water gushed forth and collected in a natural basin beneath to form the lake of Gosainkunda. Shiva threw himself down to quench his thirst, and devout Hindus today claim that the partly-submerged rock that may be seen from the lakeshore is Shiva himself, lying on a bed of serpents.

Gosainkunda is just one of several lakes trapped high in the mountains of the Gosainkund Lekh south of the Langtang Valley, above which shepherds graze vast flocks of sheep and goats during the summer months. There are four more lakes (Bhutkunda, Nagkunda, Dudhkunda and Surjekunda) on the way to the Laurebina La, and another two below (Bhairavkunda and Saraswatikunda) that are seen from the Sing Gompa trail. From the upper lakes a glorious panorama shows a line of crystal summits far off towards the Annapurnas; a line of mountains that abruptly ends with a lowland haze spreading to the south.

During the full moon festival of *Janai Purne* in July-August, thousands of Hindu pilgrims journey up from the plains to make offerings of flowers, coins and grains of rice and, placing them in leaf platters, cast them into the Gosainkunda lake. The devout then immerse themselves in the water and so gain merit. For lowland Hindus to bathe in a lake at an altitude of 4381 metres (14,373ft) must call for considerable devotion, for even in the height of summer when monsoon mists trawl the mountains the water will still be extremely cold.

103

Harka Gurung (in *Vignettes of Nepal*) tells how one faithful Hindu died in the lake when he lost his loincloth whilst bathing. Fearing to wade ashore which would only display his nudity to a group of village girls who had made the pilgrimage with him, he squatted in the chilled water, developed cramp and drowned. Few Western trekkers follow these trails in the monsoon months, and he'd be a very brave (or foolhardy) soul, who chose to immerse himself in any of these lakes during the spring or autumn trekking seasons.

*

The trek from the Trisuli Valley to the Gosainkund lakes is a short but steep two-day affair from Dhunche with an altitude difference of more than 2400 metres (7874ft), which could cause problems with acclimatisation. Most who trek here, however, do so as part of a longer expedition - either to Langtang or Helambu or both, for Gosainkund is ideally situated between the two to be seen as an obvious link, and those who have already trekked through Helambu or Langtang should be well acclimatised by the time they approach Gosainkund. Combining all three regions into one long journey of two weeks or more is to enjoy one of the classic treks of Nepal.

Two approach routes are described below. The first comes directly from Dhunche, the second from Syabru, while a south-easterly approach is given under the 'Helambu' section later in this book.

From both Dhunche in the Trisuli Valley, and Syabru at the entrance to the Langtang Valley, a steep climb above terraced fields and through forest leads to the few buildings of Sing (or Shin) Gompa where the two routes combine. There are two lodges here, a cheese factory and a simple Buddhist monastery. On the hillside above, charred and broken tree stumps give sorry evidence of deforestation.

The next day leads through a beautiful forest, then emerges to glorious views of the Langtang peaks in the north. Gaining height along a good path which rises among rhododendrons, a huge panorama begins to open out behind you. Snow-peaks stretching (it is claimed) from the Annapurnas to Manaslu and on to the Ganesh Himal and Langtang provide an amazing spectacle. From the rough lodges at Laurebinayak that panorama grows even more extensive, but the route continues to climb and soon becomes an alpine-style

belvedere trail against steep rocky crags leading directly to Gosainkunda.

The lodges at Gosainkund are all very basic, and they can be bitterly cold in November. They are usually closed during the winter (December to March) when the Laurebina La is impassable. Groups using tents must ensure they have enough fuel for cooking since Gosainkund is included in the Langtang National Park where the use of firewood is strictly forbidden.

DHUNCHE - SING GOMPA

Distance:	8 kilometres (5 miles)
Time:	5-5$^1/_2$ hours
Start altitude:	1950 metres (6398ft)
High point:	Sing Gompa (3254m: 10,676ft)
Height gain:	1304 metres (4278ft)
Accommodation:	Lodges at Sing Gompa

This particular route is normally used only by those trekkers who have come directly from Kathmandu by bus (for details of this journey refer to the section entitled 'Kathmandu-Trisuli Bazaar-Dhunche' above), and who have only a few days to spare for a very brief introduction to the hill country. But it's a strenuous start to any trek, and if you have sufficient time you'd be advised to ignore this route altogether and instead walk to Syabru (see description of the Dhunche-Bharkhu-Syabru stage under the Langtang section above), and take the Syabru to Sing Gompa alternative trail offered below. This would add another day to the trek, but it would be worth considering. However, for those who wish to take the direct route, the following outline is offered.

*   *   *

From the lodges in Dhunche walk roughly eastwards along the dirt road as far as the first hairpin bend where a signposted trail breaks away to follow the Trisuli Khola coming from the Gosainkund lakes. At this point the Trisuli is just a tributary of the main valley river, which upstream of Dhunche is known as the Bhote Kosi. The trail

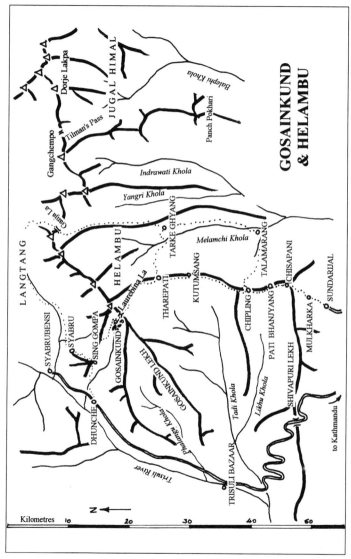

GOSAINKUND & HELAMBU

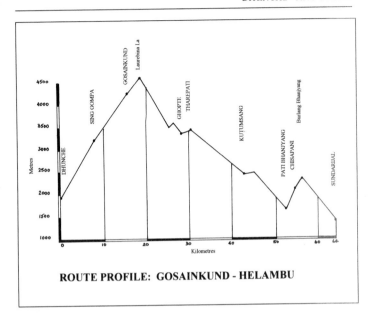

ROUTE PROFILE: GOSAINKUND - HELAMBU

eases among terraced fields, then crosses the river by a wooden bridge.

Now on the north (true right) bank of the Trisuli Khola, the way soon begins to rise steeply towards a ridge and passes through a small village (**DIMSA**?). Above this enter a lovely forest of tall rhododendron and fir trees. After about two hours you will come to a tea-house. Continue climbing to gain the ridge where there's a junction of paths. Take the right-hand option which leads past an army camp and continues to Sing Gompa.

SING GOMPA (3254m: 10,676ft) consists of a cheese factory, two lodges and a monastery. Nearby there's an apple orchard. The gompa, or monastery, is a modest building containing a statue of the Green Tara. If you visit (enquire at one of the lodges for the caretaker), don't forget to leave a donation towards its upkeep.

SYABRU - SING GOMPA

Distance:	5 kilometres (3 miles)
Time:	3-3$^{1}/_{2}$ hours
Start altitude:	2118 metres (6949ft)
High Point:	Sing Gompa (3254m: 10,676ft)
Height gain:	1138 metres (3727ft)
Accommodation:	Simple lodges en route, two lodges at Sing Gompa

This stage follows another steeply climbing path which rises over vegetated hillsides and through lovely sections of oak, pine or rhododendron forest. Views are therefore restricted for some of the way, but when you can see beyond the trees or shrubs, it's to either Langtang peaks or those of the Ganesh Himal. There are several trail junctions, particularly on the outskirts of Syabru, that could confuse the route. If in doubt check at tea-houses along the way for the trail to Sing Gompa.

* * *

At the upper end of Syabru a signpost directs the way to Chandrabari. The trail climbs past the village gompa and the school, and then eases below an Army post where there's a path junction. Take the right-hand (upper) path alongside the perimeter fence surrounding Army land, climbing quite steeply in places and twisting among lush vegetation. There are several alternative, or short-cut, trails.

After about 40 minutes come to a chorten and a simple tea-house enjoying fine views to the Ganesh peaks, plus an attractive line of mountains in Tibet, as well as Langtang summits to the north-east. Fifteen minutes later reach a second tea-house. The way continues above it and in another 15 minutes comes to **Mountain View Lodge** (1hr 10mins *accommodation, refreshments*), a simple lodge with an apple orchard nearby, and a small, wind-driven prayer-wheel on a post.

Above this lodge the way soon enters broad-leaved forest that changes to evergreen a little higher up the hillside. The trail winds steadily through, and when the forest thins, more fine views of snow-peaks are to be had. Eventually leave the forest and soon after top a

ridge at about 3200 metres (10,499ft) where there are two basic lodges perched on the narrow crest. From Syabru it will take a little over two hours to reach this point.

There's a trail junction here. The right-hand path descends to Brabal and Dhunche. Ours passes between the lodges and swings left, soon dropping to the right-hand side of the ridge where it eases into forest again. This is an enchanted evergreen forest with tall, straight-trunked trees heavily coated with moss. After a while the pines are intermingled with beautiful pink-barked rhododendrons, and there are park-like glades through which the trail works a gentle meandering course.

Three hours or so from Syabru emerge from the forest to find the skeleton trunks of dead trees stunted on the hillside ahead, and moments later arrive at the neat collection of buildings of Sing Gompa. (Just before reaching the lodges a trail cuts off to the right, signposted to Dhunche.)

SING GOMPA (3254m: 10,676ft) is little more than a couple of lodges, a cheese factory and a small, modest monastery. The stone lodges are well built, almost Western in style and of a higher standard than those beside the trail from Syabru. There's also plenty of level ground for groups who are camping. Sunset views can be spectacular.

Trekkers on the trail leading from Syabru to Sing Gompa

The few buildings of Sing Gompa with deforested slopes above

SING GOMPA - LAUREBINAYAK - GOSAINKUND

Distance:	7 kilometres (4¹/₂ miles)
Time:	4 hours
Start altitude:	3254 metres (10,676ft)
High point:	Gosainkund (4381m: 14,373ft)
Height gain:	1127 metres (3697ft)
Accommodation:	Lodges at Laurebinayak and Gosainkund

A magnificent day's trekking with outstanding views. There's quite a lot of height to gain, and if you're not sufficiently acclimatised it would be better to spend a night at Laurebinayak. Those who have already enjoyed a trek in Langtang should not suffer unduly, but anyone having come straight out from Kathmandu ought to carefully monitor any headache or feelings of nausea and take action to ensure conditions of AMS do not deteriorate.

From Sing Gompa another forest leads the way to a ridge with an extensive panorama. The trail then rises up this ridge among rhododendrons to gain the few basic lodges of Laurebinayak which command one of the great views of this corner of the Himalaya.

Above Laurebinayak the way continues to climb, but now over a broad open hillside. Crossing a ridge you then skirt a deep rocky basin on a rising traverse against steep crags before topping another crest with Gosainkund seen just below. This part of the route can be difficult or dangerous in heavy snow, and at times becomes impassable. At Gosainkund the altitude is such that night-time temperatures will be a lot lower than at Sing Gompa, especially late in the autumn; a good sleeping bag and warm clothing will therefore be essential, whether you're staying in lodges or camping.

*   *   *

From the lodges take a trail leading directly in front of the gompa and up some steps before rising among those naked, dead trees and wandering into forest. Soon emerge to a hillside flush with rhododendrons. The ridge then becomes quite alpine. The trail climbs onto the crest among tall pine trees between which you can see Langtang Lirung, Tibetan mountains with snow-glinting summits, and the Ganesh Himal too. It's a very fine trail that leads through this

111

pine forest, and in places it is paved with flat slabs of stone. Then you leave the trees behind as the path skirts the left-hand side of the ridge, once more able to enjoy magnificent views of countless snow-peaks way off to the left.

Come to a clutch of simple tea-houses at **CHALANG PATI** (3380m: 11,089ft 1hr *refreshments*) perched on the ridge which is known here as the Chalang Pati Danda. Continuing, the trail climbs straight up the ridge, which is broader now, among countless rhododendrons and with magnificent views all the way. About 45-50 minutes from Chalang Pati come onto a crest of the ridge by the few very simple lodges of **LAUREBINAYAK** (3930m: 12,894ft 2hrs *accommodation, refreshments*).

Laurebinayak can be a cold, windy site, but the panorama which stretches unhindered far off includes Manaslu, Himalchuli, Peak 29, Ganesh Himal, Paldor, the frontier range north of the Sanjen Khola, Langtangs I and II and Langtang Lirung. It is also claimed that the Annapurnas too may be seen beyond Manaslu.

From Sing Gompa to Laurebinayak the trail has been mostly broad, but above the lodges it becomes even wider, snaking its way in gentle windings up the open hillside. In places it is paved, with views unhindered by vegetation. On a high point above the lodges stands a small shrine with a collection of poles outside it. (According to Harka Gurung pilgrims leave their staves here on the way down from Gosainkund as a form of thanksgiving. He says that Laurebina means 'the place of discarded sticks'.) There's a standpipe nearby.

Then the path crosses the ridge by the remains of some stone buildings (c.4145m: 13,599ft 2hrs 45mins) and traverses along the right-hand, south, side where a route has been cut from the steep mountain wall, and with a deep drop on the right. This is a bad section for anyone tending towards vertigo! Extra care will be required if there's any snow or ice on the trail. It's a spectacular route, the path almost alpine in its construction, cut as it is against the great crags, and it undulates along the mountainside in dramatic fashion.

The gradient eases and the first of the Gosainkund lakes, Saraswatikunda, is seen below. From it a waterfall pours down to forests above Dhunche as the beginnings of the Trisuli Khola. The trail crosses a rocky spur, and a short while later the much larger second lake, Bhairavkunda, comes into view. (Note: there is some

From the trail to the Laurebina La, the lake of Gosainkunda appears to nestle in a lipped bowl of hillside

confusion as to the names and order of these lakes. Maps disagree over which is which, as do the various 'authorities' - although the main lake, Gosainkunda, is not under dispute.)

Two hours from Laurebinayak the trail climbs again, but without undue effort this time you top a short rise and there below stretches Gosainkunda with the few rough lodges and assorted low stone buildings huddled on its northern shore.

GOSAINKUND (4381m: 14,373ft) at the time of writing has three basic lodges, plus a few simple stone huts in which porters and pilgrims huddle for the night. A small Hindu shrine on the lakeside contains a *linga* and *yoni* (male and female representation), with a bell suspended outside. Gosainkunda has been a site of pilgrimage for centuries, and it is said that the Malla kings of Kathmandu had a tradition of bathing in the lake following their coronation, and of making a monetary offering to the gods here. Pilgrims still toss coins into the lake, and apparently enterprising young boys fish them out of the water at the time of the pilgrimage and thereby earn themselves some useful 'pocket money'.

113

If Gosainkund represents the turning point of your trek, and you have sufficient time and settled weather to do so, it would be worth spending a day or so exploring the surrounding hills for extensive views, not only of the long Himalayan chain of snow-peaks of the north, but across the southern lowlands too. The Laurebina La (4610m: 15,125ft), to the south-east of Gosainkund, is also well worth visiting (allow a little over an hour from the lodges). A description of this will be found in the following section, 'Gosainkund - Laurebina La - Ghopte' which is the next stage on the continuing trek to Kathmandu via Helambu.

WAYS OUT

From Gosainkund continuing route options facing the trekker may be summarised as below:

1: **Return to Dhunche** for the road back to Kathmandu. This is the quickest option, taking 1-2 days to Dhunche via Sing Gompa, followed by a day's bus ride from there. Simply reverse the trails already described above.

2: **Trek to Langtang** via Sing Gompa and Syabru. This would take about five days to reach Kyangjin, and another 3-4 days for the return down-valley to Dhunche. The route would be: Gosainkund - Sing Gompa - Syabru - Changtang - Langtang - Kyangjin. (Reverse the trail described in the opposite direction as far as Syabru, then follow directions for the Langtang trek outlined above.)

3: **Cross the Laurebina La into Helambu** for an excellent trek to Kathmandu in about 4-5 days by way of Ghopte - Tharepati - Kutumsang - Chisapani - Sundarijal. This route is described in detail under the 'Helambu' section which follows. There is an alternative option which diverts from the main trail at Tharepati and goes through the heart of Helambu by way of Melamchigaon and Tarke Ghyang. This too is described under 'Helambu' overleaf.

HELAMBU

If landscapes were sold like the sheets of characters of my boyhood, one penny plain and twopence coloured, I should go the length of twopence every day of my life.
(Robert Louis Stevenson)

Helambu (otherwise known as Helmu) is certainly what Stevenson would have called a twopence landscape. Its contrasts of immaculate terracing, rhododendron forests and incredible views north make it ideal for first-time trekkers and for those with limited time at their disposal. And when linked with routes through Langtang and over Gosainkund, it provides an unforgettable introduction or conclusion to one of Nepal's classic treks.

Close proximity to the Kathmandu Valley has given the region certain status and a degree of prosperity. In the past its attractive young women were in great demand to fill various jobs in the Rana households of the capital, especially, according to Harka Gurung, in the palace harems. But now that Rana rule has gone Helambu's value to the city is focused on the provision of water, dairy produce and the bounty of its fertile terraces. Above Sundarijal, for example, a small reservoir provides Kathmandu with a fair proportion of its drinking water, while farther east a dairy collects milk and milk products from surrounding hill farms to be transferred to the city. It's very much an agricultural land, with vast terraced hillsides growing far more than the scattered villages of Helambu could possibly need for themselves.

The population is predominantly Sherpa, although the Sherpas here are quite different from their better-known cousins of Solu-Khumbu, using a different dialect in speech, wearing different dress and following different customs. But like those of the Everest region, the Sherpas of Helambu are Buddhists; their finest gompa is Bhutanese in style, and is situated in the large village of Tarke Ghyang towards the upper reaches of the Melamchi Khola Valley.

Helambu is confined to just two main valleys, those of the Melamchi Khola and the Indrawati Khola, the two converging near Melamchi Pul Bazaar. The Indrawati is an important tributary of the Sun Kosi, but in its higher reaches is formed of the Yangri Khola and

115

Larke Khola rivers. The eastern ridge that walls the Indrawati marks the divide between Helambu and the Jugal Himal, while Helambu's western limit is drawn by a lovely series of ridges that project roughly southward from the Gosainkund Lekh. Streams draining the eastern side of this ridge system flow into the Melamchi Khola, while those that streak the western side feed the Trisuli River.

*

The main trek here follows the ridge between Sundarijal and Tharepati, either heading north with impressive views to the Langtang and Jugal peaks, or south along that crest having come from Langtang and Gosainkund. The latter direction will be described first as a continuation of those trek routes already given in detail in previous sections of this guide.

Southbound from Gosainkund to Sundarijal

After leaving Gosainkund the southbound trek crosses the Laurebina La (4610m: 15,125ft) and descends steeply to a rough lodge at Phedi before working a way over steep hillside spurs of the Thare Danda to Ghopte and Tharepati. Tharepati provides an opportunity to cut eastwards into the Helambu heartland, to the Sherpa villages of Melamchigaon and Tarke Ghyang, then south from there following the valley of the Melamchi Khola before breaking away to Pati Bhanjyang for the route out to Sundarijal and Kathmandu.

The alternative option at Tharepati, and the one most frequently taken by trekkers having come from Gosainkund, follows the ridge south through Mangengot, Kutumsang, Chipling and Pati Bhanjyang, then climbs over the Shivapuri Lekh, the ridge walling the Kathmandu Valley, in order to descend steeply to Sundarijal where a bus may be taken to Kathmandu itself.

North from Sundarijal

In reverse, the northbound route is rather more energetic and demanding for there are some long, steep climbs to be made. The first of these begins on the edge of Sundarijal, with barely any respite until you top the ridge at Burlang Bhanjyang (2438m: 7999ft), nearly a thousand metres above. From this pass, which marks the northern

rim of the Kathmandu Valley, an amazing panorama of big mountains rewards the effort of getting there.

From Burlang Bhanjyang to Pati Bhanjyang is nearly all downhill, but soon after leaving Pati Bhanjyang there begins another long uphill climb that becomes rather severe both below and above the village of Chipling. Rhododendrons nearby, and glorious terracing to the east, ensure there's plenty to enjoy on those rare occasions when the mountains are temporarily hidden.

North of Kutumsang there are no real villages along the Yurin Danda, just a few shepherds' *goths* and collections of lodges, the largest of these being at Tharepati on a windy ridge-top at 3490 metres (11,450ft). If the plan is to continue to Gosainkund and Langtang, the trail from Tharepati goes through a wild forested region with a sense of remoteness about it. It was here, between Tharepati and the simple lodge at Phedi, that Australian trekker James Scott became lost in the winter of 1991-92, and was miraculously rescued, almost dead from starvation, after spending 43 days alone. (See *Lost in the Himalayas* by James Scott and Joanne Robertson for the full story; a tale that should serve as a warning to all solo trekkers!)

From Phedi the trail to the Laurebina La and Gosainkund is very steep in places, and could be difficult in poor conditions. The crossing is usually impassable in winter.

As mentioned earlier Tharepati gives an opportunity to break away eastwards into the valley of the Melamchi Khola on a trek that visits Melamchigaon and Tarke Ghyang before returning down-valley to Pati Bhanjyang. This option provides a deeper cultural experience than the main ridge-crest trail, but views are not quite as spectacular as those enjoyed on the higher route.

GOSAINKUND - LAUREBINA LA - GHOPTE

Distance:	12 kilometres (7$^{1}/_{2}$ miles)
Time:	4$^{1}/_{2}$-5 hours
Start altitude:	4381 metres (14,373ft)
High point:	Laurebina La (4610m: 15,125ft)
Low point:	Ghopte (3430m: 11,253ft)
Height gain:	389 metres (1276ft)
Height loss:	1340 metres (4396ft)
Accommodation:	Lodges at Phedi and Ghopte

This is a much more strenuous stage than the accumulated time and distance quoted above might otherwise suggest, and is made so by the steepness of the descent from the Laurebina La (also known as the Suryakunda Pass), and by the narrow, rough trail that links Phedi with Ghopte. In snow or ice conditions, or with poor visibility, this particular section can be difficult, if not dangerous, and may well tax inexperienced trekkers.

It might be tempting when planning this stage to continue beyond Ghopte, where there are just two very basic lodges, and go as far as Tharepati (about 1$^{3}/_{4}$ hours). In good conditions, and if you're feeling fit or are in a hurry to get back to Kathmandu, that will certainly be feasible, but by the time you get there Ghopte will probably seem far enough for most trekkers.

* * *

Leaving Gosainkund the path skirts the north shore of the lake, then slants uphill at a generous gradient towards the south-east and the unseen pass. As you gain height note the distant views back to the west, beyond the lake and lodge buildings towards snowy Manaslu and its attendant peaks lining the far horizon. Other lakes soon come into view in a secretive little glen off to the right. About 45 minutes from the lodges the trail leads just to the right of a lake that may be frozen over late in the autumn, and soon after skirts another. The scenery up here is very fine; rugged high pasture, old moraines and exposed boulders, small tarns, jaunty peaklets and far views. A final lake is seen just short of the **LAUREBINA LA** (4610m: 15,125ft), which is gained in a little over an hour from Gosainkund.

It would be worth leaving rucksacks at the pass and walking up

the small hill adorned with prayer flags and cairns seen just above it, for there you will gain an even more extensive view than that enjoyed from the pass itself.

After snowfall the descent on the south-eastern side can be quite treacherous and in such cases caution is advised. The slope at first is very steep, but it eases after a while and about 45 minutes from the pass brings you to a tea-house at **BHERA GOTH** (c.4100m: 13,451ft 1hr 50mins *refreshments*). Just below this the trail forks. The left-hand option, apparently, traverses steep mountainsides and is supposed to be a shorter route to Tharepati. Its reputation is such that you should not be tempted to try this unless you have good settled weather and are guided by someone who knows the way. Instead continue on the main trail which soon descends steeply again among berberis and juniper scrub, with lots of gentians beside the trail in November. The way leads down an old moraine cone, then drops sharply to the left into a gorge-like cleft at the base of which huddles the lodge of **PHEDI** (3500m: 11,483ft 2hrs 35mins *accommodation, refreshments*).

The path decends a short steep slope below the lodge, and crosses the Tadi Khola on a log footbridge. It then picks a tortuous way along the steep left-hand flanks of the gorge. It's a rough trail requiring care, with a big drop to the right. For a while it gains and loses height with some consistency, but with a few more gentle sections too. About 45 minutes from Phedi there's another simple tea-house (3hrs 10mins *refreshments*) which is not always open, and beyond which the trail climbs in earnest. It slants up and over a succession of ridge spurs among rhododendron bushes, reaching a high point about an hour and a half from Phedi.

Over this high spur the trail descends through a brief patch of forest, then over open, stony hillsides; the trail is rough underfoot once more. Mostly down now, but with some short uphill sections, you top a final spur and overlook the rough, basic lodges of Ghopte.

GHOPTE (3430m: 11,253ft) consists of two very simple lodges and a large overhanging rock under which porters traditionally sought shelter. Accommodation here is at its most basic, and although there is a somewhat primitive atmosphere, from the lodges at night you can look out beyond the forested lower glen to the lights of Trisuli Bazaar. The buildings of Tharepati can also be seen on the ridge to the south.

GHOPTE - THAREPATI - KUTUMSANG

Distance:	14 kilometres (8$^{1}/_{2}$ miles)
Time:	5$^{1}/_{2}$ hours
Start altitude:	3430 metres (11,253ft)
High point:	Tharepati (3490m: 11,450ft)
Low point:	Kutumsang (2470m: 8104ft)
Height gain:	60 metres (197ft)
Height loss:	1020 metres (3346ft)
Accommodation:	Lodges at Tharepati, Mangengoth and Kutumsang

The big mountains having been left behind, views of snow-crowned peaks are mostly restricted throughout this stage; for the majority of the time it will be a long-ranging series of foothill ridges that dominate. But that is not to suggest the route has little in the way of scenic interest. It's a varied stage, alternating between forest and open ridge, and with a very different landscape to that experienced at either Gosainkund or in the Langtang Valley. The only true village is that of Kutumsang, for Tharepati is little more than a collection of trekkers' lodges, and Mangengoth just a couple of **bhatti** *and an Army checkpost. In between are a few goths or shelters that are deserted for much of the year. There remains a sense of remoteness, although the steady descent is a constant reminder that each step on the way south brings you closer to habitation.*

With loss of altitude vegetation becomes more abundant, but rhododendrons remain a constant feature. In springtime there's vivid colour everywhere, and meadows are starred with flowers.

The first section of the trail from Ghopte to Tharepati can be difficult after snow, or extremely greasy following heavy rainfall. Being a narrow trail it may be easily lost in poor visibility, and especially so when snow obliterates its course. It crosses a series of rib-like spurs and boulder slopes, and involves some height gain. But once you leave the Tharepati lodges behind the way becomes increasingly clear and the trail more heavily used as practically all trekkers exploring Helambu come this way, whether or not they include Gosainkund in the itinerary.

* * *

The trail drops steeply from Ghopte's lodges, then resumes its up and down course along the mountainside. It's a rough path threading a way among rhododendron trees, up sudden rocky sections and over short boulder slopes, but then out of trees the lodges of Tharepati are clearly seen on the crest of the hill ahead.

THAREPATI (3490m: 11,450ft 1hr 45mins *accommodation, refreshments*) is perched on, or a little below, the ridge crest. As you reach the first of the lodges a secondary trail cuts off to the left (east) and is signposted to Melamchigaon. This route is outlined later. The trail to Kutumsang continues to the upper lodges, then curves to the right, briefly along the crest from where you can see down to the left (east) into the Melamchi Khola Valley, then slips down the right-hand flank among rhododendrons. The path now is a good, broad, well-padded trail that makes for comfortable walking.

Soon return to the ridge at a small saddle with wide views, then go down some stone steps and along the ridge crest. About one hour from Tharepati pass a couple of rough stone *goths*, beyond which the way descends to another saddle and a junction of trails. The left-hand option provides an alternative way down to Melamchigaon, while the right-hand trail will eventually lead to Kutumsang.

Tharepati lodge sign

Without anything overly strenuous on this stage of the trek, in about an hour and a half from Tharepati the right-hand path brings you to the meadowland clearing of **MANGENGOTH** (3150m: 10,335ft 3hrs 15mins *accommodation, refreshments*) with its Army checkpost set off to the right, linked by a path to two basic lodges. It is important to enter details of your trekking permit in a book at the checkpost. The soldier on duty will also need to look at your National Park entry permit.

Beyond the lodges the trail can be seen climbing to a dip in the wooded ridge. It follows an obvious line to it, but on arrival there you find this is merely a false saddle, for you descend slightly to pass more *goths*, then climb again through a fold of hillside to the main saddle (3285m: 10,777ft) which is marked by a large pile of stones and prayer flags.

Descend through magnificent rhododendron forest, the big pink trunks gnarled and twisted and hung about with Spanish moss. An hour from Mangengoth the forest opens to a broad hillside from where it seems all the land is folding down towards the unseen Kathmandu Valley. The trail here is heavily eroded and the deep ruts, scoured by the monsoon rains, make for uncomfortable walking. Happily it does not last. Below the worst of the eroded section the trail leads past an isolated lodge (4$^{1/2}$hrs *accommodation, refreshments*) and camping ground.

More delightful forest lies between this lodge and Kutumsang, and on the way through the village shows itself below at times between the trees. Descending still, come to the first part of Kutumsang where there's a National Park office, a mani wall and the village school. There's also a trail junction by the mani wall. Ignore the path which drops to the right and continue ahead, passing alongside the school, then among rhododendrons again, before coming to the main part of the village set upon a saddle in the ridge overlooking terraced fields on either side and glorious views to snow- and ice-capped mountains of the Jugal Himal in the north-east.

KUTUMSANG (2470m: 8104ft) has plenty of lodges beside the trail. It's a somewhat scruffy little village inhabited largely by Tamangs who tend the fertile terraces and graze their flocks in the pastures up towards Mangengoth. Morning views towards Urkinmang, Dorje Lakpa and their neighbours can be breathtaking.

Morning light bathes the houses of Kutumsang

KUTUMSANG -CHIPLING - PATI BHANJYANG - CHISAPANI

Distance:	13 kilometres (8 miles)
Time:	5¹/₂-6 hours
Start altitude:	2470 metres (8104ft)
Low point:	Pati Bhanjyang (1768m: 5801ft)
Height gain:	813 metres (2667ft)
Height loss:	1088 metres (3570ft)
Accommodation:	Lodges at Gul Bhanjyang, Chipling, Pati Bhanjyang and Chisapani

This stage makes for a magnificent day's trekking. It's an energetic route with plenty of height gain and loss, but the foothill country is quite enchanting. Here is a face of Nepal with particular attraction. Gone are the high bare mountains, and in their place thousands of trim terraces have been layered down the hillsides wherever you look; there are small villages strung out along the ridge crests, isolated houses and farms tied to the land. Ascents

123

and descents alike can be demanding, but if you've an eye for a tended, cared-for land, you'll love this day's walk.

A word of warning before you set out may not go amiss in regard to the southern end of this stage. Chisapani is an ugly hybrid lodge village, now reached by a dirt road. The lodges are comfortable enough, their menus offering assorted styles of food and their small shops stocked with goods unseen since you left Dhunche. And views are tremendous. However, as in several other roadhead villages serving popular trekking routes, it does sometimes have a few rogues hanging around and you should make a point of not leaving your baggage unattended. If you're staying in one of the hotels, keep it locked in your room for safe-keeping. You may even consider the alternative of stopping an hour or so short of Chisapani, at Pati Bhanjyang where there's also accommodation, and pass through Chisapani next day on the way out to Sundarijal and Kathmandu. But what you'd miss by so doing, however, would be glorious evening skies over the high mountains of the north, and the splendour of early morning.

* * *

Out of Kutumsang the trail passes along the ridge crest, rising to the south while views behind grow in extent the higher you go - views to shapely snow mountains barring the horizon to both north-east and north-west, and down to vast terraced hillsides, the best of which are seen bordering the Melamchi Khola Valley. About 30 minutes from the village come to a solitary tea-house on the ridge, then descend past the **Dragon Lodge** (35mins *accommodation, refreshments*), a handsome stone-built hotel with a neat camping space in front. Beyond this the trail is rough and eroded, descending a slope towards Gul Bhanjyang, seen below. There is a second lodge by a stream a few minutes' walk from the Dragon Lodge.

A little over an hour from Kutumsang enter the narrow main street of **GUL BHANJYANG** (2142m: 7028ft 1hr 15mins *accommodation, refreshments*) which is lined with lodges and shops. This Tamang village is strung along the ridge, with terracing below and charming foothill views to enjoy. At the far end of the street go uphill again and pass a small stupa at the top of a flight of steps, then continue beyond it to find another lodge about half an hour from the village, followed by a few houses and a second stupa.

Continue up the ridge, then cross to the right-hand side by a lone tea-house. Vegetation is quite lush on this western side, and the gradient more gentle for a while. On coming to a brief col the way recrosses to the left-hand (eastern) side, climbs again and returns to the western flank once more among trees, this time largely oak forest.

A little under three hours from Kutumsang come onto a ridge spur of the Namche Danda at 2453 metres (8048ft), and then begin the long descent to Chipling, at first down a seemingly endless flight of stone-paved steps that give way lower down to a rough and eroded trail. In half an hour from the Namche Danda spur enter **CHIPLING** (2165m: 7103ft 3hrs 15mins *accommodation, refreshments*), a small village clustered on a ridge overlooking an amazing stepped landscape. There are two simple lodges and a school.

After passing through the village the trail continues to descend, this time in steep zig-zags among terraces. A few houses are set beside the trail, most of them attractive stone-built dwellings with a neat thatch and a few hens scratching in the dust outside. It takes about 40 minutes to reach **THANA BHANJYANG** (1780m: 5840ft 4hrs *refreshments*), a small saddle in the hills with a couple of tea-houses and a junction of three trails. Take the central path of the three. This is a delightful trail that skirts the right-hand side of the hill ahead and makes a gentle traverse along its western slope. It passes several groups of houses overlooking a splay of terraced hillsides, and soon begins a short descent into **PATI BHANJYANG** (1768m: 5801ft 4hrs 30mins *accommodation, refreshments*). As its name suggests, the village occupies another saddle in the hills. A single, very narrow street is lined with houses, shops and lodges, and with a police checkpost at the far end. The residents of Pati Bhanjyang are Brahmin or Chhetri, Hindu castes, and you will notice a small Hindu shrine in the village street as you pass through.

Just beyond the police checkpost the path divides. Take the right-hand option and begin the 400 metre (1312ft) climb to Chisapani. At times this is a very steep trail. Sometimes you're climbing through deep, dank gullies, but as height is gained so the countryside opens and you emerge onto an almost moorland-like broad ridge with extensive views. Along this ridge a little over an hour from Pati Bhanjyang come to Chisapani and a dirt road.

CHISAPANI (2194m: 7198ft) has several unattractive lodges

Morning views from Chisapani are spectacular

clustered beside the road. At the time of writing not one bears any resemblance to the local architecture of a Helambu hill village, but instead the place better resembles a roadhead shanty somewhere on the plains of India. That being said, standards of accommodation and food on offer are better than in most traditional Helambu lodges. No doubt more will be established here as the road increases in importance.

In spite of a distinct lack of architectural merit, Chisapani enjoys one of the great views of Nepal, looking north across the foothill ridges to the great wall of the Gosainkund Lekh to the upper snows of Langtang peaks. West of these rise the far distant Annapurnas, Manaslu, and Ganesh Himal, while to the east the Jugal Himal looks magnificent, with Dorje Lakpa and Lenpo Gang standing proud among a rich company of huge white peaks swelling ever eastward.

CHISAPANI - BURLANG BHANJYANG - SUNDARIJAL

Distance:	10 kilometres (6 miles)
Time:	3-3½ hours
Start altitude:	2194 metres (7198ft)
High point:	Burlang Bhangjyang (2438m: 7999ft)
Low point:	Sundarijal (1463m: 4799ft)
Height gain:	244 metres (801ft)
Height loss:	975 metres (3200ft)
Accommodation:	Lodges at Mulkharka and Sundarijal

It's quite feasible to have breakfast in Chisapani and lunch in Kathmandu, for this final stage is not overly time-consuming, yet the trek retains interest to the very end. There's a small amount of height to gain at the start, during which it's tempting to stop every few minutes to enjoy 'one last magnificent view' of the Himalayan wall in the north; then there's a steady descent to the roadhead at Sundarijal, with the Kathmandu Valley in sight for much of the way. There is, of course, a world of difference between the two, but both have their charm and help make this an enjoyable walk throughout.

The Shivapuri Lekh above Chisapani has an unfortunate reputation for banditry. Whilst I am unaware of any recent attacks on trekkers, it would be wise to take care on this stage, and the earlier warning against trekking alone is particularly relevant here. It should be stressed, however, that the incidence of theft and violence in Nepal is much less than in the so-called 'civilised' West, but where trekkers have been targeted it has usually been within a day or so of a roadhead. It would be prudent to keep valuables out of sight. Do not allow this warning to spoil what is potentially a superb morning's walk, but simply remain vigilant as you go.

*   *   *

From the lodges at Chisapani walk south along the dirt road, and when it curves to the left break away on a rutted path that climbs ahead up a slope. At this point take a moment to enjoy the stunning view back to the north where the far horizon is a wild sea of big snow-capped peaks. The climb follows a steady gradient and reaches the minor pass of Chepu Bhanjyang in about 40 minutes. This is little

more than a narrow cleft in the wooded ridge, beyond which the trail descends a few metres, then follows a delightful level section, as gentle as an English park, winding among trees and shrubs, then opening to allow another brief study of the distant mountains. The trail rises again, then veers to the right, and suddenly you have one last chance to enjoy an impressive panorama: Langtang peaks, the Gosainkund Lekh and the various ridges crossed since the Laurebina La, recognising tiny villages in which you may have stayed, or at least walked through...Feast your eyes, for in a moment they will be gone.

Ten minutes from Chepu Bhanjyang the trail rises through a groove, or sunken track, and brings you directly to the pass of **BURLANG BHANJYANG** (2438m: 7999ft 50mins) marked by a pile of stones almost hidden by vegetation. As forest rises all around there are no views to be had, so begin the descent through another deep groove carved by thousands of feet and aided by the annual monsoon rains. This sunken track, between mossy banks overhung with vegetation, is but the first of many on this descent.

About 15 minutes from the pass emerge from tree cover, and there below lies the Kathmandu Valley with blue distant hills rising on the far side. The way descends through open terraces (unworked now that the village of Chaurabas is no more), then returns once more to forest and another sunken track. Eventually this leads to a neat area of cropped grass and an avenue of pines by a Nepalese Army post.

Yet another short sunken section brings you to a few farms, with terraces put to use, and banana trees throwing shade. In about two hours from Chisapani come to the first houses of the large, strung-out Tamang village of **MULKHARKA** (1768m: 5800ft 2hrs *accommodation, refreshments*). The village consists mainly of farmhouses, but there are several lodges and tea-houses too. The trail through is sometimes eased by paved steps, sometimes on broad concrete steps, at times rough stones or rutted dirt.

Come to a dirt road by the **Karma Restaurant and Lodge** (*accommodation, refreshments*). This is the same road that leads to Chisapani. Cross over and remain on the continuing footpath which descends to the small reservoir that serves Kathmandu. Beyond this a short staircase of steps leads to a broad and easy trail. Pass another Army post and soon come to more steps. Just before reaching a large water pipe note the Hindu *linga* and *yoni* symbols beneath a large

Above Gosainkund a high rolling landscape reveals more distant views
The houses of Gul Bhanjyang stretch in a line along a saddle in the ridge

Chipling; thatched houses perched on a ridge crest

The foothill country of Helambu, with the Jugal Himal beyond,
as seen from above Chisapani

overhanging rock on the right. Follow the water pipe down to Sundarijal.

SUNDARIJAL (1463m: 4799ft) is a large and untidy village at the roadhead, about 15 kilometres (9^1/$_2$ miles) from Kathmandu. There are lodges, tea-houses, shops and daily buses to the capital. Most buses terminate at Bhodnath (Boudha), reached in about an hour from Sundarijal. About 10 minutes' walk from the bus park there's a first-aid post and a place for reporting missing people; also the Himalayan Rescue Dog Training Centre which was set up in 1989 by Dutchman Ingo Schnabel.

SUNDARIJAL TO GOSAINKUND

The northward journey through Helambu to Gosainkund and the Langtang Valley is justifiably popular and vies with the southbound route as one of Central Nepal's classic treks, particularly as trekking in this direction provides almost constant views to the big mountains. As the southbound route has been described in some detail above, the trail from Sundarijal to Gosainkund is outlined here with a little less emphasis on detail. As suggested earlier, trekking south to north is more energetic and demanding than in the opposite direction, for there's a difference in altitude between Sundarijal and the Laurebina La of 3147 metres (10,326ft), and with plenty of taxing ascents on the way. There are sufficient lodges throughout to enable independent trekkers to achieve this route without resorting to the full service of porters, tents etc, while group trekkers will find no shortage of camp grounds in villages and near isolated lodges. It's a well-trekked route, but above Tharepati the trail is a little thin and can be difficult in or after snowfall.

From Sundarijal to Gosainkund allow 5-6 days, depending on individual fitness and rate of acclimatisation.

SUNDARIJAL - BURLANG BHANJYANG - CHISAPANI

Distance:	10 kilometres (6 miles)
Time:	4-4^1/$_2$ hours
High point:	Burlang Bhanjyang (2438m: 7999ft)
Height gain:	975 metres (3200ft)
Height loss:	244 metres (801ft)
Accommodation:	Lodges at Mulkharka and Chisapani

On this first stage trekkers should be wary of making an obvious display of their valuables. In the past one or two incidents of banditry have taken place in the forested area above Mulkharka, and although I am unaware of any recent incidents (and such cases are extremely rare in Nepal) all who trek there should be aware of the problem and remain vigilant. Walking alone is not a good idea.

Sundarijal is reached in a little under an hour from Kathmandu by either bus or taxi. From the bus park in Sundarijal (this is just a turn-round point at the end of the road) the route begins by following a track alongside a large water pipe, then up steps past a number of houses following the pipeline uphill. Eventually come to a small reservoir (1585m: 5200ft) which provides much of Kathmandu's drinking water. Cross the dam and continue along an obvious trail that leads up to a dirt road near the **Karma Restaurant and Lodge** (*accommodation, refreshments*).

The continuing trail passes alongside the lodge and maintains its climb to the large, strung-out Tamang village of **MULKHARKA** (1768m: 5800ft *accommodation, refreshments*). Hundreds of steps take the trail steeply through this village, passing houses, farms and simple lodges with pumpkins in their gardens and banana trees casting shade.

Above Mulkharka the trail climbs on towards the ridge of the Shivapuri Lekh and passes through a deeply sunken section before coming to an Army post. There is much forest cover between here and the pass, and large sections of trail go through more sunken grooves scoured by the monsoon rains. This region is contained within the conservation area of the Shivapuri Watershed and Wild Life Reserve.

BURLANG BHANJYANG (2438m: 7999ft) is heavily wooded so there are no views from the pass itself. A short distance beyond, however, the trail leads to a spectacular panorama of distant mountain peaks making a long snow-bound crest on the northern horizon, before forest conceals the view again. Cross a second, minor, pass, **CHEPU BHANJYANG** and begin to descend to Chisapani, soon emerging from forest to a clear view of the distant mountain wall.

CHISAPANI (2194m: 7198ft) has several unattractive lodges whose standards of accommodation and food, however, should be perfectly acceptable. The dirt road crossed below Mulkharka passes through the village. Views to the Jugal Himal are particularly impressive.

CHISAPANI - PATI BHANJYANG - CHIPLING - KUTUMSANG

Distance:	13 kilometres (8 miles)
Time:	6-6$^{1}/_{2}$ hours
High point:	Kutumsang (2470m: 8104ft)
Height gain:	1088 metres (3570ft)
Height loss:	813 metres (2667ft)
Accommodation:	Lodges at Pati Bhanjyang, Chipling, Gul Bhanjyang and Kutumsang

At first the trail crosses broad open countryside, then begins the descent to Pati Bhanjyang, part of the way being through yet more deep sunken grooves that can be slippery following rain. **PATI BHANJYANG** (1768m: 5801ft *accommodation, refreshments*) is reached in less than an hour. A somewhat scruffy village nestling in a saddle in the hills, with tea-houses and lodges lining the single street. There is a police checkpost at its entrance.

On the northern side of the village the trail slants round the left flank of the ridge. An alternative path here veers to the right and gives an opportunity for trekkers to visit Talamarang and the Melamchi Khola Valley (described in reverse under details for the Helambu Circuit). Ignore this option and keep on the left of the ridge, and in about half an hour come to another saddle, **THANA BHANJYANG** (1780m: 5840ft *refreshments*) where there are two tea-houses.

Now the climb begins in earnest, a steep trail working its way up a tremendous terraced hillside, at times on a rising traverse, at others in steep zig-zags to gain the small village of **CHIPLING** (2165m: 7103ft *accommodation, refreshments*), set on a ridge spur with a few simple lodges. Chipling does not mark the top of the climb, though, but merely a half-way point, for the trail continues beyond the northern edge of the village, at first up an eroded slope, then on a never-ending staircase of stone steps.

Cross a wooded spur of the Namche Danda at 2453 metres (8048ft), and begin the gentle descent of the far side, making for the Tamang village of Gul Bhanjyang. Passing several tea-houses, isolated lodges and a couple of stupas, eventually reach **GUL BHANJYANG**

(2142m: 7028ft *accommodation, refreshments*). There are several shops in the village street. Kutumsang is about two hours from here.

Beyond Gul Bhanjyang the trail rises over open meadows to pass a couple of lodges, the second of which, **Dragon Lodge** (*accommodation, refreshments*), is a smart, stone-built hotel with a trim camp ground in front. From here climb the ridge to a tea-house and continue northward, soon sloping down a little to Kutumsang.

KUTUMSANG (2470m: 8104ft) has plenty of lodges and camp grounds, and enjoys fine views of the Jugal Himal.

KUTUMSANG - THAREPATI

Distance:	11 kilometres (7 miles)
Time:	5-5^1/$_2$ hours
High point:	Tharepati (3490m: 11,450ft)
Height gain:	960 metres (3150ft)
Accommodation:	Lodges at Mangengoth and Kutumsang

Continue trekking north along the ridge. On the edge of the village pass a mani wall and a National Park checkpost, then rise through prickly oak forest on an eroded trail. The forest changes to rhododendron and fir as you gain height, and eventually you emerge to an open hillside and an isolated lodge. Above this erosion is extremely bad, the trail being cut into very deep ruts that make uncomfortable walking.

Once more return to rhododendron forest near some *goths*. Now the trail is much better under foot, and the gradient eases until a final uphill pull brings you to a saddle in the ridge (3285m: 10,777ft) marked by a huge pile of stones and prayer flags.

Go down the easy slope beyond and a few minutes later arrive at the two simple lodges of **MANGENGOTH** (3150m: 10,335ft *accommodation, refreshments*) situated in a meadowland clearing. Just beyond them there's an Army checkpost where permits must be shown.

The trail resumes, still heading north, and climbs among trees and rhododendrons. In and out of forest, and passing an occasional *goth*, the way brings you to another brief saddle and a junction of paths.

The right-hand option leads to Melamchigaon and the upper Helambu region, while the left-hand trail continues along the ridge to Tharepati.

THAREPATI (3490m: 11,450ft *accommodation, refreshments*) consists of a number of lodges set either on the very ridge-top, or just below it. Views are splendid, but the site is notoriously cold and windy so you'll need a decent sleeping bag if you plan to spend a night here.

THAREPATI - GHOPTE - PHEDI

Distance:	9 kilometres (5$^{1}/_{2}$ miles)
Time:	3-3$^{1}/_{2}$ hours
High point:	3690 metres (12,106ft)
Height gain:	280 metres (919ft)
Accommodation:	Lodges at Ghopte and Phedi

Descend the western side of the ridge to the lower lodges of Tharepati (the eastern side descends to the Melamchi Khola) and follow a narrow trail through forests on the flanks of the Thare Danda. The way descends steep rocky sections, crosses minor streams and climbs over projecting ribs before twisting up to a large overhanging rock and the two simple lodges at **GHOPTE** (3430m: 11,253ft *accommodation, refreshments*).

Above these climb to a ridge spur, through more forest and along a rough section of trail. The way climbs again and works a route along the steep mountainside high above the valley of the Tadi Khola. This part of the route can be difficult in poor conditions, and dangerous when the trail is hidden beneath fresh snow. There is a solitary tea-house between Ghopte and Phedi, but it is not always open so don't rely on being able to get refreshment there.

The high point on this stage is a ridge spur approached through rhododendrons. Once over the route resumes its up and down course and eventually descends to a log footbridge over the Tadi Khola in a narrow gorge. Once across this the trail climbs steeply again, but almost immediately brings you to the rough lodge at Phedi.

PHEDI (3500m: 11,483ft *accommodation, refreshments*) means 'at the foot of the hill' which is an apt description of this rather gloomy place.

PHEDI - LAUREBINA LA - GOSAINKUND

Distance:	6 kilometres (4 miles)
Time:	4-4$^{1}/_{2}$ hours
High point:	Laurebina La (4610m: 15,125ft)
Height gain:	1110 metres (3642ft)
Height loss:	229 metres (751ft)
Accommodation:	Lodges at Gosainkund

From the lodge a very steep trail twists its way up the hillside to an old moraine cone, and continues at a strenuous gradient to gain a tea-house at **BHERA GOTH** (c.4100m: 13,451ft *refreshments*), the only chance of refreshment before the lodges of Gosainkund.

Above this the path continues to climb, but now a little easier than before. There will be a few ribbons of streams to cross higher up, then another steep pull all the way to the pass of **LAUREBINA LA** (4610m: 15,125ft). There is a small hill just above the pass, topped with a large cairn and prayer flags, and it would be worth climbing to the top to enjoy magnificent views, both back the way you have just come, and ahead towards Gosainkund and the distant crest of the Himalaya.

The path is clearly defined down to Gosainkund. It crosses a high rough pastureland, weaves around the edge of two or three lakes, then looks down onto Gosainkunda, the main lake itself, sacred to Hindus. Easing down to the lodges the trail skirts the northern shore with good views all the way.

GOSAINKUND (4381m: 14,373ft) has just three basic lodges, a few rough stone hutments and a Hindu shrine.

To trek from here to Kyangjin in the Langtang Valley would take about five days. An outline of this route, and other ways out, will be found above under the 'Gosainkund' section.

THE HELAMBU CIRCUIT

A very fine trek of a week or so may be had by combining the ridge route already described between Sundarijal and Tharepati with trails that lead through the valley of the Melamchi Khola. Such a circuit enables trekkers to gain a better understanding of the way of life of Nepalese hillfolk; it explores villages and their rich agricultural terraces, visits gompas and draws upon the spirituality of the Helambu Sherpas for much of its charm, while the lower valley villages are inhabited by Newari, Brahmin and Chhetri peoples.

The main circuit has as its pivot the village of Pati Bhanjyang, a long day's walk from Sundarijal. Being a circular trek it could be walked in either direction, but it is preferable to tackle this particular route clockwise, to strike northward first along the high ridge section in order to have those wonderful Himalayan views to entice you on, then return south through the valley of the Melamchi Khola on the second half of the trek. The alternative, anti-clockwise, circuit would lead to Tarke Ghyang in relative ease in about three short day stages from Pati Bhanjyang, perhaps stopping overnight in such villages as Talamarang and Thimbu.

It's a trek equally suited to tented, organised groups, with their caravans of porters, as to independent trekkers relying on tea-houses and lodges for food and accommodation. Trails are mostly clearly defined and may be followed in all seasons, although in the event of heavy snowfall the ridge trail above Kutumsang may be difficult or even dangerous in places.

The initial western ridge-back portion of the trek, starting from the roadhead in Sundarijal, has already been described in the foregoing pages. Three days should suffice in order to reach the break-off point at Tharepati, during which time the trek will have covered some 34 kilometres (21 miles) in linear distance, and an accumulated height gain of 3023 metres (9920ft). There will be a few steep uphill sections to face, but also many magnificent viewpoints from which to study snow-laden summits of the Langtang and Jugal Himals.

A summary of these stages reads as follows:

1: Sundarijal-Burlang Bhanjyang-Chisapani - a route that climbs

out of the Kathmandu Valley to the Shivapuri Lekh (the ridge forming the north rim of the valley) at Burlang Bhanjyang, then descends a short and easy slope to Chisapani. Since Pati Bhanjyang is less than an hour from Chisapani, some trekkers prefer to continue to that village.

2: Chisapani-Pati Bhanjyang-Chipling-Kutumsang - some very demanding 'staircase' sections on the trail leading to Chipling, and from there to a spur of the Namche Danda. From the head of this long ascent the route then continues along the ridge crest virtually all the way to Kutumsang.

3: Kutumsang-Tharepati - a more remote feeling to this stage as there are no real villages after Kutumsang. There are, however, a few tea-houses and simple lodges. Long stretches of forest reduce prospects of mountain views, but Tharepati overlooks much fine country.

From Tharepati the Helambu Circuit breaks away from the Gosainkund trail and heads to the east, to Melamchigaon and Tarke Ghyang. An outline description of this stage follows:

4: Tharepati-Melamchigaon-Tarke Ghyang - The original trail to Melamchigaon left the ridge at a small saddle below and to the south of Tharepati, but there is now an alternative way signposted from the northern end of the lodge settlement. It descends the ridge's eastern flank, at first quite steeply through a hillside groove, and winds through forests of conifer, rhododendron and oak, crosses a tributary of the Melamchi Khola, then climbs to the Sherpa village of **MELAMCHIGAON** (2560m: 8399ft) where there are a number of lodges. The village has an electricity supply, and a gompa standing among a sentry-line of prayer flags.

On the opposite side of the Melamchi Khola, on a hillside shelf enjoying a similar altitude to Melamchigaon, stands the neighbouring village of Tarke Ghyang, but to reach it involves further descent of more than 600 metres (1969ft) to the river. Leave the village through a *kani*, or entrance chorten, and follow the trail down for about an hour. Cross the Melamchi Khola on a suspension bridge, then climb the eastern slope, an ascent that crosses more tributary streams before reaching the attractive village of Tarke Ghyang, the largest in all Helambu.

TARKE GHYANG (2560m: 8399ft) is a neat and prosperous Sherpa settlement whose stone houses share the same power supply

as that of Melamchigaon. There are several lodges, some of whose owners occasionally meet prospective guests on the trail with assurances that theirs is the best hotel in town. The fine Bhutanese style gompa was built in 1969 to replace an earlier monastery of 1727. If you have time it would be worth spending at least two nights here. The village and its surroundings repay exploration, while to the north a minor peak on the Yangri Danda at an altitude of 3771 metres (12,372ft) provides spectacular mountain views and makes a worthwhile day's excursion.

There's a choice of two routes south from Tarke Ghyang. The standard Helambu Circuit trail is described first:

5: Tarke Ghyang-Kakani-Thimbu-Talamarang - A clear path descends the western flank of the ridge dividing the valleys of the Melamchi and Indrawati Kholas, heading south to **KAKANI** and **THIMBU**, both rather scattered Sherpa villages. Below Thimbu the way passes through sub-tropical forest and into rice-growing country. Almost 1300 metres (4265ft) lower than Tarke Ghyang, **KIUL** is the next village, its houses set among terraced fields.

After leaving Kiul cross the second suspension bridge over the Melamchi Khola and soon come to **MAHANKAL**. There is a road here that has fallen into disrepair since being cut by floods further down-valley. Follow the road (shortcuts available to avoid long bends) as far as **TALAMARANG** (960m: 3150ft); now at the roadhead it may be possible to beg a lift on a truck to Kathmandu if required.

6: Talamarang-Thakani-Pati Bhanjyang - On the edge of the village a suspension bridge crosses the Talamarang Khola. The trail to Pati Bhanjyang follows the south bank of this tributary stream among rice terraces heading west. For much of the way it keeps close to the stream, the path improving as the gradient steepens on the approach to the ridge, on the west side of which the upper, outward, route led between Pati Bhanjyang and Thana Bhanjyang. Eventually come to the village of **THAKANI** (Baruwa Thulo Thakani; 1890m: 6201ft), then wander along the ridge heading roughly southward, and soon descend to **PATI BHANJYANG** (1768m: 5801ft), snug in a saddle on the ridge. At this point you close the Helambu Circuit. To return to Sundarijal and Kathmandu follow the trail already described via Chisapani.

The alternative route from Tarke Ghyang remains high to begin with, then descends to the Melamchi Khola Valley south of Talamarang, at Melamchi Pul Bazaar near the confluence with the Indrawati Khola.

5a: Tarke Ghyang-Shermathang - A short day's trek, and without any great climbs or descents to tackle, it usually finishes at Shermathang because there are several lodges and good views. The trail leaves Tarke Ghyang near the Tarke Ghyang Guest House and heads south, following power lines to **PARACHIN**. The way then curves into the head of a tributary glen, on the far side of which may be seen the attractive village of **GANGJWAL**, at a marginally lower elevation than Tarke Ghyang. Now the way descends a little, then contours south-eastward along the hillside, crossing streams and a landslide area to reach **SHERMATHANG** (otherwise known as Sarmathang; 2621m: 8599ft).

6a: Shermathang-Melamchi Pul Bazaar - The Palchok Danda narrows at its southern end into a wedge squeezed by the converging valleys of the Melamchi and Indrawati Kholas, and the descent to Melamchi Pul Bazaar follows the ridge all the way. There are a few villages and, in the upper part of the trek, lots of chortens and a gompa at Kakani as a constant reminder that this is still Buddhist country, though that will change once you reach the valley bed. The trail leads through **KAKANI**, then steeply down to **DUBACHAUR**, 1100 metres (3609ft) below Shermathang. There is a further knee-twitching descent of a little over 600 metres (1969ft) to gain the valley at the confluence of the Indrawati and Melamchi Kholas. Cross the Melamchi Khola by suspension bridge and soon enter **MELAMCHI PUL BAZAAR** (846m: 2776ft).

From here it's possible to return to Kathmandu by bus via the road that goes down the right bank of the Indrawati to Panchkal on the Kathmandu-Kodari Highway, or alternatively continue trekking to Nagarkot and Bhaktapur. This option involves a 5 kilometre (3 mile) walk down-valley along the road to Bahunepati, followed by a trail that climbs via Tangla Bhare to Nagarkot on the eastern rim of the Kathmandu Valley, famed for its sunrise and sunset views. Nagarkot is linked by road with Bhaktapur.

OTHER TREK IDEAS

Those routes described in some detail are, naturally, the classic treks of the region and as a result they've become justifiably popular. But anyone with experience of trekking in Nepal will appreciate that there are numerous alternative trails, following secondary ridge crests or winding through tributary valleys, that would repay exploration. Even the poorest maps indicate the existence of countless trails and villages that rarely, if ever, see a foreign face, and to wander these routes can be a magical experience. A rudimentary knowledge of the language would be a distinct advantage along untrekked trails, for there will be no lodges and unless you carry a tent and plenty of food, you will need to stay in private houses wherever possible. Not all trails shown on the maps are clear on the ground, however, and in many cases it would be prudent to have a local guide with you. Study all available maps in detail and discuss ideas with a Nepali guide before setting out.

The Jugal Himal

To the east of Helambu the Jugal Himal, crowned by such magnificent peaks as Dorje Lakpa and Lenpo Gang, is sparsely populated, and anyone planning to trek there would need to be self-sufficient. The best point of access is the village of Chautara, the administrative centre for Helambu district, which is reached by road from Kathmandu. North of Chautara a long ridge system marks a divide between the valleys of the Indrawati Khola and the Balephi Khola, and a series of trails provides possibilities for a trek along it to the holy lakes of Panch Pokhari.

Such a trek could be combined with a return through Helambu, demanding about two weeks in all. The route is roughly as follows:

From **CHAUTARA** trek roughly northward along the dividing ridge for about three days to reach the cluster of five sacred lakes known as **PANCH POKHARI**. Backtrack along the ridge until a trail descends steeply to the Indrawati on the western side. Cross the **INDRAWATI**, and the **YANGRI KHOLA**, then climb past two gompas on the way to the **YANGRI LA** which provides easy access to **TARKE GHYANG**. From there follow trails already described to

TALAMARANG, PATI BHANJYANG and across the Shivapuri Lekh to **SUNDARIJAL**.

The Ganesh Himal

West of the Trisuli Valley the Ganesh Himal forms a high mountain block that appears so appealing, particularly when viewed from Laurebinayak below Gosainkund. With the 'trekking peak' of Paldor attracting climbers, the way to it from Dhunche or Syabrubensi has become reasonably well-known. Unfortunately the dirt road leading to the lead and zinc mines at Somdang has devalued some of this approach.

The Ganesh foothills are crossed by few trails and a local guide who knows the country will be needed to lead a way across. Parties must be self-sufficient as there are no trekkers' lodges.

West of Somdang runs the ridge of the **TIRU DANDA**, from which magnificent views reveal the Manaslu Himal rising to the west on the far side of the Buri Gandaki Valley. The ridge is ablaze with rhododendrons in springtime, and there is a trail leading south along it, which allows a fine, rarely-travelled trek to be made that ends either through the valley of the Salankhu Khola to **BETRAWATI** or via lovely terraced farmland of the Sami Khola Valley to **TRISULI BAZAAR**. By combining this route with a north-bound trek through Helambu and Gosainkund, a splendid 15-16 day trek could be achieved.

An alternative trek across the Ganesh Himal could be created by wandering south along the **TIRU DANDA** as mentioned above as far as the **SINGLA BHANJYANG**, then descend westward into the valley of the **ANKHU KHOLA**. This valley flows into the Buri Gandaki, from which trails cross the hills to **GORKHA** (bus to Kathmandu); or you could join the Gorkha-Trisuli trade route eastward to **TRISULI BAZAAR**. The Mandala trekking map, *Kathmandu to Manaslu Ganesh Himal*, though sparse on detail, provides scope for dreaming. See also *Adventure Nepal* by Diana Penny Sherpani for basic route outlines.

APPENDIX A: USEFUL ADDRESSES

1: Selected Overseas Missions of the Nepalese Government:

Embassies:

UK
12a Kensington Palace Gardens
London W8 4QU
(Tel: 0171 229 1594)

USA
2131 Leroy Place
Washington
DC 20008 (Tel: 202 6674550)

France
7 rue de Washington
75008 Paris (Tel: 43592861)

Germany
Im-Hag 15
Bad Godesberg 2
D-5300 Bonn (Tel: 0228 343097)

Consulates:

USA
820 Second Avenue
Suite 202
New York
NY 10017 (Tel: 212 3704188)

473 Jackson Street
San Francisco
CA 94111
(Tel: 415 4341111)

Canada
310 Dupont Street
Toronto
Ontario (Tel: 416 9687252)

Australia
870 Military Road
Suite 1 Strand Centre
Mosman, Sydney
NSW 2088 (Tel: 9603565)

2: Selected Foreign Missions in Nepal:

British Embassy
Lainchaur
Kathmandu
(Tel: 411789/410583)

American Embassy
Pani Pokhari
Kathmandu
(Tel: 411179/411601)

Australian Embassy
Bhat Bhatani
Kathmandu (Tel: 411578)

The following countries also have Embassies located in or near Kathmandu:

China: Baluwatar
Germany: Kantipath
Israel: Lazimpat
Japan: Pani Pokhari
Korea (South): Tahachal
Thailand: Thapathali

France: Lazimpat
India: Lainchaur
Italy: Baluwatar
Korea (North): Patan
Pakistan: Pani Pokhari

The following countries have Kathmandu-based Consulates:

Austria: Kupondole
Denmark: Kantipath
Netherlands: Kumaripati
Switzerland: Jawalakhel

Belgium: Lazimpat
Finland: Khichpokhari
Sweden: Khichpokhari

In addition the following Cultural Centres are based in Kathmandu:

The British Council
Kantipath (Tel: 211305)

French Cultural Centre
Bag Bazar (Tel: 214326)

United States Information
  Service
New Road (Tel: 211250)

3: Map Suppliers:

Edward Stanford Ltd
12-14 Long Acre
London
WC2E 9LP

Bradt Enterprises Inc
95 Harvey Street
Cambridge
MA 02140 USA

Michael Chessler Books
PO Box 2436
Evergreen
CO 80439 USA

Note: there are also many booksellers in Kathmandu who stock trekking maps for the Langtang and Helambu regions.

4: Health Advice for Travellers:

MASTA (Medical Advisory Service for Travellers Abroad)
Keppel Street, London WC1E 7HT
(Telephone Travellers' Health Line: 01891 224100)

APPENDIX B: TREKKING AGENCIES

The following list of agents, both in Kathmandu and the United Kingdom, is not a comprehensive one, but is offered as a guide only. Many other agents exist, and as businesses come and go, and occasionally change their names, some of those actually listed might not survive this edition. *Please note that mention of any trekking agent in this book should not be seen as an endorsement of that company's services.*

1: Nepal-based Agents:

Note: to telephone Nepal from the UK dial 00 (International code), then 977 + 1 (for Kathmandu) followed by the individual number.

Ang Rita Trek & Expedition
PO Box 7232
Thamel, Kathmandu
(Tel: 226577 Fax: 977 1 229459

Highland Sherpa Trekking
PO Box 3597
Jyatha Tole, Kathmandu
(Tel: 226487)

Himalayan Explorers
PO Box 1737
Thamel, Kathmandu
(Tel: 226142)

Mountain Travel
Box 170
Narayan Chour, Naxal
(Tel: 414508)

Mt Kailash Paradise Trekking
PO Box 5343
Kathmandu
(Tel: 475744 Fax: 977 1 471103)

Sherpa Cooperative Trekking
Box 1338
Durbar Marg, Kathmandu
(Tel: 224068)

2: Trekking Agents Based in the United Kingdom:

Bufo Ventures
3 Elim Grove
Windermere LA23 2JN
(Tel: 015394 45445)

Classic Nepal
33 Metro Avenue
Newton, Derbyshire DE55 5UF
(Tel: 01773 873497)

Exodus
9 Weir Road
London SW12 0LT
(Tel: 0181 675 5550)

Explorasia
Sloan Square House
Holbein Place
London SW1W 8NS
(Tel: 0171 973 0482)

Explore Worldwide
1 Frederick Street
Aldershot
Hants GU11 1LQ
(Tel: 01252 344161)

High Places
Globe Works
Penistone Road
Sheffield S6 3AE
(Tel: 0114 2757500)

Karakoram Experience
32 Lake Road
Keswick
Cumbria CA12 5DQ
(Tel: 017687 73966)

Out There Trekking
62 Nettleham Road
Sheffield S8 8SX
(Tel: 0114 2588508)

Roama Travel
Shroton
Blandford
Dorset DT11 8QW
(Tel: 01258 860298)

Specialist Trekking
Cooperative
Chapel House
Low Cotehill
Nr Carlisle
Cumbria CA4 0EL
(Tel: 01228 562368)

Guerba Expeditions
101 Eden Vale Road
Westbury
Wilts BA13 3QX
(Tel: 01373 826611)

Himalayan Kingdoms
20 The Mall
Clifton
Bristol BS8 4DR
(Tel: 0117 9237163)

Nepal Trekking
10 Swinburne Street
Hull HU8 8LY
(Tel: 01482 703135)

Ramblers Holidays
Box 43
Welwyn Garden City
Herts AL8 6PQ
(Tel: 01707 331133)

Sherpa Expeditions
131a Heston Road
Hounslow
Middx TW5 0RD
(Tel: 0181 577 7187)

Worldwide Journeys &
    Expeditions
8 Comeragh Road
London W14 9HP
(Tel: 0171 3818638)

APPENDIX C: GLOSSARY

Although it is quite possible to trek the main trails of the Langtang and Helambu regions speaking only English, a little effort to communicate with Nepalis in their own language shows good-will and will be amply repaid. If you are travelling with an organised group plenty of opportunities will arise to practise a few words and phrases with your trek crew and porters. Tea-house trekkers will find that some attempt to speak the language of their hosts will be appreciated by lodge-keepers and owners of tea-houses along the trail, while those who employ a porter-guide will discover that mutual language-exchange is a valuable bonus to the day-to-day pleasures of the trek. Locals who meet and work with Europeans are invariably eager to expand their vocabulary, and are usually happy to offer some instruction in Nepali in return for help given in English.

Whilst the Tamangs and Sherpas of Langtang and Helambu have their own language which they speak among themselves - as do many other ethnic groups - Nepali is the one unifying language of the country. The following glossary lists a selection of words that may be useful along the way. However, there are a few Nepali phrasebooks and dictionaries available that would be worth consulting, in addition to Stephen Bezruchka's highly recommended language tape and accompanying book, *Nepali for Trekkers* (The Mountaineers, 1991) which provides an essential guide to pronunciation and grammar. Lonely Planet publish a small, lightweight *Nepal Phrasebook* that would easily fit into a shirt pocket for instant use on the trail.

aaja	-	today
aalu	-	potatoes
ama	-	mother
ava	-	father
baato	-	trail
baayaan	-	left (direction)
banthanti	-	the place in the forest
bazaar	-	market
bhanjyang	-	foothill pass
bhat	-	cooked rice

bhatti	-	traditional inn or guest-house
bholi	-	tomorrow
Bhot	-	Tibet
Bhotyia	-	Buddhist people of mountain Nepal
bistaari	-	slowly
chang	-	home-made beer
chapaati	-	unleavened bread (see also roti)
charpi	-	toilet
chaulki	-	police post
chautaara	-	trailside resting place
chini	-	sugar
chiso paani	-	cold water
chiyaa	-	tea
chorpen	-	temple guardian
chorten	-	Buddhist shrine, like an elaborate cairn
daahine	-	right (direction)
daal bhat	-	staple meal of Nepal: rice with lentil sauce
danda	-	ridge
deurali	-	pass on a ridge
dhai	-	yoghurt
dhara	-	waterspout
dharmsala	-	pilgrims' rest house
dherai	-	many, much
dokan	-	shop (see also pasal)
doko	-	porter's conical load-carrying basket
drangka	-	stream (see also nadi)
dudh	-	milk
gaau	-	village (see also gaon)
gaon	-	village (see also gaau)
ghar	-	house (see also khangba)
gompa	-	Buddhist temple or monastery
goth	-	herdsman's shelter
hijo	-	yesterday
himal	-	snow mountain
kang	-	mountain
kani	-	covered archway, or entrance chorten, covered with Buddhist motifs
kata	-	Buddhist scarf

khaana	-	food
khangba	-	house (see also ghar)
kharka	-	high pasture
khola	-	river
khukari	-	Gurkha knife with curved blade
kosi	-	river
kot	-	fortress
kund	-	lake (see also pokhari and tal)
la	-	high pass (Tibetan)
lama	-	Buddhist monk or priest
lekh	-	hill, or foothill ridge
lho	-	south
maasu	-	meat
maati baato	-	upper trail
mandir	-	Hindu temple
mani	-	Buddhist prayer; from the mantra 'Om Mani Padme Hum'
mani wall	-	stone wall carved with Buddhist mantras
mantra	-	religious incantation
momo	-	stuffed savoury pastry, or dumpling
naalaa	-	small stream
nadi	-	stream (Hindi: see also drangka)
namaskar	-	more polite form of namaste
namaste	-	traditional greeting; it means 'I salute the god within you'
namlo	-	porter's headband
nun	-	salt
nup	-	west
paani	-	water (see also chiso paani, taato paani and umaleko paani)
panchayat	-	system of area council
pasal	-	shop (see also dokan)
phedi	-	literally 'the place at the foot of the hill'
phul	-	egg
pokhari	-	lake (see also kund and tal)
puja	-	religious offering, or prayer
pul	-	bridge (see also sangu)
raamro	-	good

raamro chhaina	-	not good
rakshi	-	distilled spirit, made from grain
ri	-	peak
Rimpoche	-	reincarnated priest
roti	-	bread (see also chapaati)
sadhu	-	Hindu ascetic
sangu	-	bridge (see also pul)
satu	-	flour
shaligram	-	ammonite
shar	-	east
Sherpa	-	ethnic people of Solu-Khumbu; also from upper Helambu
Sherpani	-	female Sherpa
sidha	-	straight ahead (direction)
sirdar	-	man in charge of trek crew
stupa	-	large chorten
suntala	-	orange (fruit)
taato paani	-	hot water
tal	-	lake (see also kund and pokhari)
Thakali	-	people of the Thak Khola, the upper region of the Kali Gandaki
thanka	-	Buddhist scroll painting
thanti	-	place
thukpa	-	noodle soup
thulo	-	big
trisul	-	trident symbol of followers of Shiva
tsampa	-	roasted barley flour
tsho	-	lake
ukaalo	-	steep uphill
umaleko paani	-	boiled water
yersa	-	collection of herdsmen's shelters or summer settlement

Days of the Week

Aitobaar	-	Sunday	Bihibaar	-	Thursday
Sombaar	-	Monday	Sukrobaar	-	Friday
Mangalbaar	-	Tuesday	Sanibaar	-	Saturday
Budhbaar	-	Wednesday			

Numbers

1	-	ek	25	-	pachhis
2	-	dui	30	-	tis
3	-	tin	35	-	paitis
4	-	char	40	-	chaalis
5	-	paanch	45	-	paitaalis
6	-	chha	50	-	pachaas
7	-	saat	55	-	pachpanna
8	-	aath	60	-	saathi
9	-	nau	65	-	paisatthi
10	-	das	70	-	sattari
11	-	eghaara	75	-	pachahattar
12	-	baahra	80	-	ashi
13	-	tehra	85	-	pachaasi
14	-	chaudha	90	-	nabbe
15	-	pandhra	95	-	panchaanaabbe
16	-	sohra	100	-	ek sae
17	-	satra	1000	-	ek hajaar
18	-	athaara	$1/2$	-	aadha
19	-	unnaais	$1\frac{1}{2}$	-	dedh
20	-	bis			

BIBLIOGRAPHY

There are many books on Nepal, but surprisingly few with regard to trekking in the areas covered by this guide. Those that do are of course included in the list below. Several have a wider scope, but all contain information relevant to trekkers intending to visit Langtang, Gosainkund or Helambu. Inevitably some are out of print and unobtainable in the West except, perhaps, through public libraries. But many bookshops in Kathmandu stock an admirable selection of new, old and reprinted volumes, and will be worth investigating if you cannot obtain what you require at home.

1: General Tourist Guides:

The number of general guides to Nepal seems to grow each year. Perhaps the best and most comprehensive on the market at present is:

Insight Guide: Nepal edited by Hans Höfer (APA Publications). Expert contributions, both textual and photographic, give this regularly-updated book an air of authority.

Others, with similar emphasis on photographic appeal, include *The Insider's Guide to Nepal* by Brian Tetley (Moorland Publishing Co 1991) and *Nepal* (Nelles Guides published by Nelles Verlag/Robertson McCarta 1990).

Nepal: The Rough Guide by David Reed (Rough Guides/Penguin Books 1993) and *Nepal - A Travel Survival Kit* by Tony Wheeler and Richard Everist (Lonely Planet 1993) both offer lots of practical no-nonsense information on getting around Nepal, and include some trekking information.

Not a tourist guide as such, the following large-format book is packed with an assortment of information and photographs gleaned from the author's wide-ranging travels. *Nepal: The Kingdom of the Himalayas* by Toni Hagen (Kümmerly and Frey 1980) is the definitive work on the people and geography of the country, and is highly recommended. Hagen was the first man to be given the freedom to explore the whole of Nepal and as such his knowledge, gleaned over

a period of eight years, must be considered unique.

In a different vein, *Vignettes of Nepal* by Harka Gurung (Sajha Prakashan, Kathmandu 1980) covers much of the country on foot, including a brief visit to Langtang, Gosainkund and Helambu. The author, a native of Lamjung, has held a number of government posts, and the book is an account of his travels made mostly in the course of his work. Interesting insights by a Nepali with a love of his country.

2: Trekking:

Most trekking guides to Nepal attempt to cover as many areas as possible. Each one contains plenty of interest and practical use, but for the majority of trekkers whose visit concentrates on just one route or one region only, there will inevitably be large passages of unused material.

Trekking in Nepal by Stephen Bezruchka (Cordee / The Mountaineers - 6th edition 1991) is *the* classic trekker's guide. Packed with information, it is a gem of a book. Sensitively written and regularly revised, the author's commitment to the country and his concern for the people is a shining example to all who follow in his footsteps. Anyone planning to visit Nepal should study this book before leaving home.

Trekking in the Nepal Himalaya by Stan Armington (Lonely Planet - 6th edition 1994). Another weighty guide to a number of trekking regions, including those areas covered by the present book. The author has spent many years leading trekking parties in the Himalaya, and lives in Kathmandu. The latest edition contains plenty of up-to-the-minute information and an excellent chapter devoted to health and safety contributed by Dr David Shlim of the CIWEC clinic, Kathmandu.

Trekking in Nepal, West Tibet and Bhutan by Hugh Swift (Sierra Club / Hodder & Stoughton 1989) provides an interesting overview of trekking possibilities in these three countries. It seeks to cover too much territory to give precise detail, but makes enjoyable reading nonetheless. A much more personal book than the previous two, it is enlivened with anecdotes that really make you want to pull on your boots and go.

Trekking in Nepal by Toru Nakano (Springfield Books 1990) has a

strong photographic content, and some of the illustrations are particularly striking. It will remind you to take a camera and plenty of film.

Adventure Treks: Nepal by Bill O'Connor (Crowood Press/Cicerone Press 1990). Not a route guidebook as such, it consists of a series of personal narratives describing a variety of treks, and manages to convey some of the magic - as well as some of the frustrations - of trekking in Nepal.

The Trekking Peaks of Nepal by Bill O'Connor (Crowood Press 1989/1991). This companion volume to *Adventure Treks* is, perhaps, of more practical value - even if you have no ambition to climb. Brief details of major trekking routes, and some obscure ones, are given, as well as the main purpose of the book, which is to outline possibilities for climbing on all 18 nominated trekking peaks. Plenty of black and white illustrations.

Adventure Nepal by Diana Penny Sherpani (Bufo Ventures 1991) is a planning guide for independent trekkers. No detailed route descriptions, but plenty of good sound advice throughout. Married to a Sherpa, the author runs her own trekking company which also organises the bi-ennial Everest Marathon.

Lost in the Himalayas by James Scott and Joanne Robertson (Lothian Books 1993) tells the remarkable true story of Scott's ordeal when he became lost between Ghopte and Phedi during the winter of 1991/92, and was rescued after 43 days, almost dead through starvation. A salutary lesson for all.

3: Mountains & Mountaineering:

Nepal Himalaya by H.W.Tilman (Cambridge University Press 1952; now included in the collection *The Seven Mountain Travel Books* published by Diadem/The Mountaineers 1983) is in a league of its own. Tilman was the first Western mountaineer to gain permission to visit Nepal, and the account of his journey to Langtang in 1949 cannot be recommended too highly to anyone planning a trek there. Read it before you go, and again when you return home. It's a gem.

Collins Guide to Mountains and Mountaineering by John Cleare (Collins1979) contains a chapter giving a brief overview of the

mountaineering history and potential of the Langtang and Jugal Himals.

4: Anthropology & Natural History:

Birds of Nepal by Fleming, Fleming and Bangdel (Avalok 1984). A comprehensive field guide, richly illustrated.

A Birdwatcher's Guide to Nepal by Carol Inskipp (Prion 1988)

Butterflies of Nepal by Colin Smith (Tecpress 1989)

Wildlife of Nepal by T.B.Shrestha (Tribhuvan University)

Concise Flowers of the Himalaya by Oleg Polunin and Adam Stainton (Oxford University Press 1987). Polunin was with Tilman in Langtang in 1949.

Himalayan Flowers and Trees by Dorothy Mierow and Tirtha Shrestha (Sahayogi Prakashan, Kathmandu 1978). A useful pocket-sized guide.

People of Nepal by Dor Bahadur Bista (Ratna Pustak Bhandar - 5th edition 1987). Background information on a number of ethnic groups of Nepal.

The Festivals of Nepal by Mary M.Anderson (George Allen & Unwin 1971). Limited to the Kathmandu Valley, but of interest.

CICERONE GUIDES

Cicerone publish a wide range of reliable guides to walking and climbing abroad

FRANCE, BELGIUM & LUXEMBOURG

THE BRITTANY COASTAL PATH
CHAMONIX MONT BLANC
- A Walking Guide
THE CORSICAN HIGH LEVEL ROUTE: GR20
FRENCH ROCK
THE PYRENEAN TRAIL: GR10
THE RLS (Stevenson) TRAIL
ROCK CLIMBS IN BELGIUM & LUXEMBOURG
ROCK CLIMBS IN THE VERDON
TOUR OF MONT BLANC
TOUR OF THE OISANS: GR54
TOUR OF THE QUEYRAS
WALKING IN THE ARDENNES
WALKING THE FRENCH ALPS: GR5
WALKING THE FRENCH GORGES (Provence)
WALKING IN THE HAUTE SAVOIE
WALKING IN THE TARENTAISE & BEAUFORTAIN ALPS
WALKS IN VOLCANO COUNTRY (Auvergne)
THE WAY OF ST JAMES: GR65

FRANCE / SPAIN

WALKS AND CLIMBS IN THE PYRENEES
ROCK CLIMBS IN THE PYRENEES

SPAIN & PORTUGAL

WALKING IN THE ALGARVE
ANDALUSIAN ROCK CLIMBS
BIRDWATCHING IN MALLORCA
ROCK CLIMBS IN MAJORCA
COSTA BLANCA CLIMBS

MOUNTAIN WALKS ON THE COSTA BLANCA
THE MOUNTAINS OF CENTRAL SPAIN
WALKING IN MALLORCA
WALKING IN THE SIERRA NEVADA
WALKS & CLIMBS IN THE PICOS DE EUROPA
THE WAY OF ST JAMES: SPAIN

SWITZERLAND including adjacent parts of France and Italy

THE ALPINE PASS ROUTE
THE BERNESE ALPS
CENTRAL SWITZERLAND
CHAMONIX TO ZERMATT The Walker's Haute Route
WALKS IN THE ENGADINE
THE GRAND TOUR OF MONTE ROSA (inc Italy)
THE JURA - Walking the High Route and Winter Ski Traverses
WALKING IN TICINO
THE VALAIS - A Walking Guide

GERMANY / AUSTRIA / EASTERN EUROPE

HUT-TO-HUT IN THE STUBAI ALPS
THE HIGH TATRAS
THE KALKALPEN TRAVERSE
KING LUDWIG WAY
KLETTERSTEIG - Scrambles
MOUNTAIN WALKING IN AUSTRIA
WALKING IN THE BLACK FOREST
WALKING IN THE HARZ MOUNTAINS
WALKING IN THE SALZKAMMERGUT

Other guides are constantly being added to the Cicerone List.
Available from bookshops, outdoor equipment shops or direct (send for price list)
from CICERONE, 2 POLICE SQUARE, MILNTHORPE, CUMBRIA, LA7 7PY

CICERONE GUIDES

Cicerone publish a wide range of reliable guides to walking and climbing abroad

ITALY & SLOVENIA
ALTA VIA - High Level Walks in the Dolomites
THE CENTRAL APENNINES OF ITALY
CLASSIC CLIMBS IN THE DOLOMITES
THE GRAND TOUR OF MONTE ROSA inc Switzerland))
ITALIAN ROCK - Rock Climbs in Northern Italy
VIA FERRATA - Scrambles in the Dolomites
WALKING IN THE CENTRAL ITALIAN ALPS
WALKING IN THE DOLOMITES
WALKS IN THE JULIAN ALPS

MEDITERRANEAN COUNTRIES
THE ATLAS MOUNTAINS
CRETE: Off the beaten track
WALKING IN CYPRUS
THE MOUNTAINS OF GREECE
THE MOUNTAINS OF TURKEY
TREKS & CLIMBS IN WADI RUM, JORDAN
THE ALA DAG - Climbs & Treks (Turkey)

HIMALAYA & OTHER COUNTRIES
ADVENTURE TREKS - W. N. AMERICA
ADVENTURE TREKS - NEPAL
ANNAPURNA - A Trekker's Guide
EVEREST - A Trekker's Guide
LANGTANG, GOSAINKUND & HELAMBU - A Trekker's Guide
MOUNTAIN WALKING IN AFRICA 1: KENYA

ROCK CLIMBS IN HONG KONG
TREKKING IN THE CAUCAUSUS
CLASSIC TRAMPS IN NEW ZEALAND

GENERAL OUTDOOR BOOKS
THE ADVENTURE ALTERNATIVE
ENCYCLOPAEDIA OF MOUNTAINEERING
FAMILY CAMPING
FIRST AID FOR HILLWALKERS
THE HILL WALKERS MANUAL
LIMESTONE -100 BEST CLIMBS IN BRITAIN
MOUNTAIN WEATHER
MOUNTAINEERING LITERATURE
MODERN ALPINE CLIMBING
MODERN SNOW & ICE TECHNIQUES
ROPE TECHNIQUES IN MOUNTAINEERING

CANOEING
CANOEIST'S GUIDE TO THE NORTH EAST
SNOWDONIA WILD WATER, SEA & SURF
WILDWATER CANOEING

CARTOON BOOKS
ON FOOT & FINGER
ON MORE FEET & FINGERS
LAUGHS ALONG THE PENNINE WAY
THE WALKERS

Also a full range of British guidebooks to walking - from short family walks, day walks to long distance trails, biking, scrambling, ice-climbing, rock climbing and canoeing

---

*Other guides are constantly being added to the Cicerone List.
Available from bookshops, outdoor equipment shops or direct (send for price list)
from CICERONE, 2 POLICE SQUARE, MILNTHORPE, CUMBRIA, LA7 7PY*

Printed by CARNMOR PRINT & DESIGN
95-97 LONDON ROAD, PRESTON, LANCASHIRE, UK.